THE FLORIDA
PLANNING GUIDE

FLORIDAESTATEPLANNING.COM

Published and printed in the United States of America

ISBN-13: 978-1508555155
ISBN-10: 150855515X

The information in this book is not intended to provide legal advice to the reader. No attorney-client relationship exists without an express written engagement between attorney and client. The reader is strongly advised to engage the services of a qualified attorney, CPA, and financial advisor as may be necessary. The author and publisher expressly disclaim any responsibility for any liability, loss, or risk, personal or otherwise, which is incurred as a consequence, directly or indirectly, of the use and application of any of the contents of this book.

Book editing by DJ Wik

Table of Contents

DOES MY ESTATE PLAN NEED A FLORIDA UPDATE?

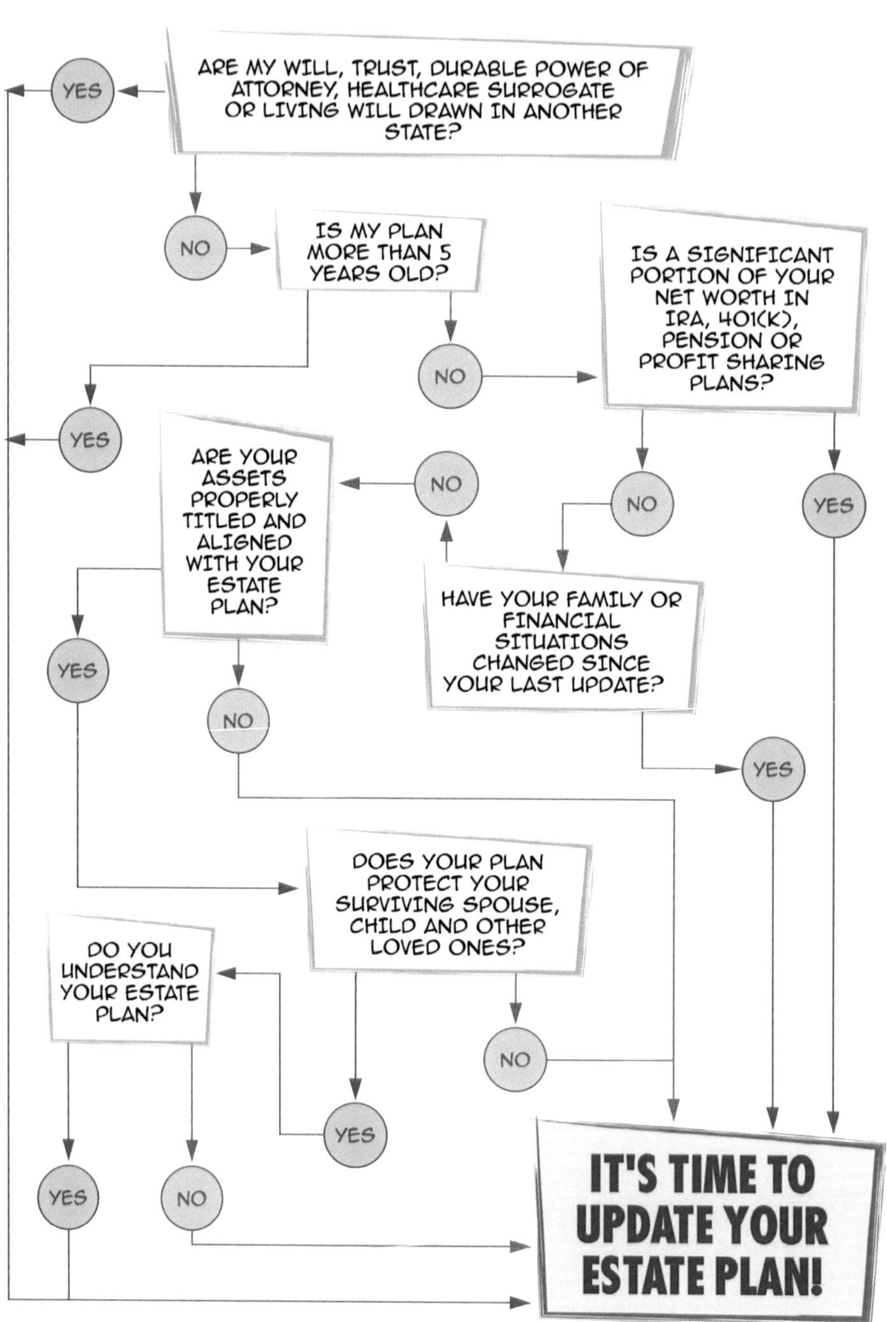

Preface

Welcome to Florida

So you're a Florida resident, or perhaps you're considering Florida residency. Congratulations! Thousands just like you move here every week. Perhaps you've been a resident of Florida for several years. Eventually you hear that you need to update your estate plan.

You've procrastinated.

After all, who wants to talk about their own demise? You've moved here to ***live*** for crying out loud, not to ***die!*** Yet, the thought still gnaws at you. You don't want to leave your loved one's in a bind, but you don't know where to begin.

You've found the right book.

In these pages you're going to read about the advantages to Florida residency, which will not only benefit your loved ones you leave behind, but could very well benefit you for the rest of your life. You'll learn how to maximize those advantages by creating an up-to-date Florida based estate plan. You'll also read about various strategies in your estate plan you may have not considered before.

How's that possible? Because no one ever told you about the opportunities.

You'll learn the difference between revocable living trusts and wills, and where one might be better than the other. In these pages I explain how the legal differences between the states will likely have a real economic effect on you and your loved ones. Check out floridaestateplanning.com/moreguide for a list comparing the residency and tax laws of all 50 states. You can look up your current (or former) home state to see whether becoming a Florida resident would be advantageous for you.

Becoming a Florida resident is quite easy, you'll see.

The hard part is escaping your former state's taxing authorities. We'll look at these issues together. I also share important information about your current or former state's taxing authorities, and how they want to keep a grip firmly around your wallet.

Even if your northern attorney has told you your plan is fine for Florida, I'm going to show you why it's probably not. I don't mean to criticize his advice, but I've seen too many assertions by my client's former attorneys, even the ones also licensed in Florida, to not point out what issues arise with many out-of-state-documents. These issues can cause real problems and are easily rectified by a knowledgeable professional who knows exactly what to look for.

Does your current estate plan wrap a protective sheath around your spouse, children and grandchildren, or will the inheritance you leave them become subject to the claims of future and divorcing spouses, creditors and predators? I discuss basic legal strategies to use that can achieve these goals. My suspicion is your current estate plan does not fully and adequately adopt these strategies.

If you already have a revocable living trust, will your assets avoid the probate process? Again, my guess is that many of your assets won't. This is because ***your assets must be transferred into your revocable living trust*** to avoid the probate process. Many new clients who visit me ***never completed this important step*** of the estate planning process, mainly because they were given a sheet of instructions without much guidance. You'll learn how our trademarked estate planning process – The Family Estate & Legacy Program® takes care of this problem and raises the other issues I've mentioned here.

Once you update your estate plan under The Family Estate & Legacy Program®, you'll be part of a Client Care program that serves to never let your plan fall out of date again.

In the epilogue I'll show you how to begin updating your estate plan. We believe you'll enjoy the process, finding clarity and comfort. How am I so confident that these assertions will come true?

My name is Craig R. Hersch, and I am a Florida Bar Board Certified Wills, Trusts & Estates attorney, practicing since 1989. I also hold my license as a Florida CPA, and I was instrumental in the formation and sit on the board of directors of a private trust company. I'm unique in the sense that I have real life experience as an entrepreneur who has practiced law extensively, and has seen from the inside how trust companies consider discretionary distribution requests when clients have established third party trusts for their loved ones.

I've built a team of highly qualified professionals around me who use my trademarked estate planning process designed to help you find the plan that meets your needs.

So please do discover for yourself how an up-to-date estate plan can benefit you during your life, and your loved ones you leave behind.

While every effort is made to convey the most current information at the time I write these chapters, the estate, trust, and tax laws are changing constantly. Because this book is only intended to be a broad overview of the issues individuals face when deciding upon state residence and estate plans, many of the details, caveats, and exceptions to the general rules that may apply to specific situations are intentionally omitted.

This book does not serve as legal advice, and no attorney/client relationship may be inferred without an express agreement between you and the author and/or his law firm. Similarly, existing clients of the author's law firm may not rely on statements made in this book. Before acting on any statement contained herein, you should always consult with a qualified professional to assess your individual facts and circumstances.

I welcome your comments, questions, and criticisms—and especially your kudos!

Please feel free to reach me at:

Craig R. Hersch
Florida Bar Attorney Board Certified Wills, Trusts & Estates Specialist; CPA
Sheppard Law Firm
9100 College Pointe Court
Fort Myers, FL 33919
239-334-1141
www.floridaestateplanning.com/moreguide
www.floridaestateplanning.com
hersch@sheppardlawfirm.com
twitter: FLTrustLaw
Facebook: The Sheppard Law Firm

Chapter One

The Advantages of Florida Residency

I get the question "Is Florida residency right for me?" almost daily in my estate planning practice. Retirees raise this question most often as they generally have the freedom to select a home state. Who doesn't look forward to watching sunsets on the beach, playing in foursomes on the golf course, boating on warm waters, and all the plethora of activities that living in Florida provides?

Many retirees who have lived their lives, spent their careers, and raised their families somewhere else often hear that Florida residency can be favorable, but they're not sure it's right for them. After years of slogging through dreary weather each October through May, they're ready to take advantage of the good life.

Moving on to Florida is often regarded as a reward for a life well lived.

Naturally many of my clients have maintained two residences. I've always thought it was interesting to examine the evolution of a typical client's journey from residing in another state to become a Florida resident. I'll illustrate this with the story of "Ed and Alice" from Ohio.

While raising their family, for many years Ed and Alice vacationed in Florida relaxing on the beach and experiencing amazing moments at the Orlando theme parks. They discovered quaint communities such as Sanibel, Naples, Delray, Homosassa Springs and Winter Park. Ed and Alice promised each other that when they got the kids off the payroll they'd buy a Florida residence to escape the frigid, gray, wet Ohio winters.

That time arrived.

Their children had been brought up and started families of their own. Free of the daily commitments of raising a family, Ed and Alice purchased a beautiful seaside town house in a Florida gated community. Each year from January through April before heading back to Ohio, Alice enjoyed golfing and playing bridge with her new friends while Ed attended spring training baseball games with his fellow sports fan buddies.

At first to not miss their grandchildren growing up, Ed and Alice maintained their Ohio home spending eight months of the year there, attending little league baseball games, dance recitals, and graduations. The grandchildren became busy with their high school friends and then went off to college. Ed and Alice formed lasting friendships in Florida, progressively spending less time in Ohio practically splitting their time between the two residences. While they truly enjoyed the holidays and family life cycle events in their old hometown, Ed and Alice increasingly wanted to spend time in the Sunshine State.

During a cocktail party hosted by one of their friends, someone brought up the issue of Florida residency and estate planning. Ed and Alice heard that there are many economic advantages to Florida residency. To their surprise, many of their friends had already established residency here. An estate planning attorney was recommended, and they began the journey towards a new primary residence.

Their first inquiries centered on whether what they heard about the benefits of Florida residency are true. They are.

Florida Tax Advantages

Florida does not have any individual state income tax, estate tax, inheritance tax or intangible tax. This usually means immediate tax savings on everything from the sale of stocks, bonds and mutual funds to withdrawals from IRA and 401(k) accounts to the receipt of annuities and pensions. While Florida residents, like everyone else in the United States, pay federal taxes there are no additional state level taxes. And this is unlikely to be changed. The Florida Legislature can't do it without voters approving a constitutional amendment.

This can mean thousands of dollars in tax savings.

Ed and Alice now pay up to 5.3% Ohio state income tax on top of what the federal government imposes. Assume that they have over $150,000 of taxable income, and they can save $8,000 of additional state level income tax by becoming a Florida resident.

It's no wonder everyone in Ed and Alice's community became Florida residents in short order. "Max and Melinda" from Minnesota became Florida residents when they realized their state income tax of over 8% meant annual income tax savings exceeding $10,000. "Ned and Nancy" from New York saved almost $25,000 on an 11% marginal rate of state and local income taxes that would have otherwise been owed on their IRA withdrawals.

Florida residents also enjoy property tax savings. Assuming one is a Florida resident as of January 1st, a homestead property tax exemption can be declared on one's primary residence. This can lead to a reduction of the taxable value of one's homestead up to $50,000. Moreover, the Save Our Homes Property Tax Assessment Cap ("SOH") limits the amount that one's homestead can increase in assessed value to no more than 3% regardless of that year's actual appreciation. Over the course of several years, the homestead property tax exemption and the SOH limitations can result in thousands of dollars of tax savings.

Comparing Florida to almost any northern state that most of our residents are from is a no-brainer. There are so many benefits to becoming a Florida resident. You can get a comparison of all 50 states' income tax rates at floridaestateplanning.com/moreguide.

Becoming a Florida Resident

Exactly how to become a Florida resident? There are a variety of factors, including being registered to vote in Florida, obtaining a Florida driver's license, and giving up your driver's license from any other state would be important. Register and title your car in Florida. If you don't drive, you can obtain a Florida identification card. A detailed checklist can be found at floridaestateplanning.com/moreguide.

Submitting a declaration of domicile and declaring your residence as your homestead works to declare your Florida residency. If there is a declaration of homestead in your former home state, and if you still own a residence there, renouncing your homestead status there is necessary. A list at floridaestateplanning.com/moreguide reviews the steps necessary to claim the valuable Florida homestead exemption and the Save Our Homes property tax assessment cap.

Your federal tax return should list Florida as your residence. If you no longer have any taxable income in your former home state, filing a "Final Return" with that state's department of revenue will help.

Having your primary physician in Florida and updating your estate plan to Florida law all works towards establishing Florida residency as well.

You might believe that it looks relatively easy to become a Florida resident, and it is. What's more problematic is severing the legal ties with your former state's taxing authority. That's the subject of the next chapter.

KEY TAKEAWAYS

> FLORIDA RESIDENTS PAY NO STATE INCOME TAX

> FLORIDA RESIDENTS PAY NO STATE ESTATE OR INHERITANCE TAX

> FLORIDA RESIDENTS PAY NO STATE INTANGIBLE TAX

> FLORIDA HOMESTEAD STATUS SAVES ON PROPERTY TAXES

> THE FLORIDA SAVE OUR HOMES PROPERTY TAX ASSESSMENT CAP SAVES ADDITIONAL PROPERTY TAXES

> DECLARING FLORIDA RESIDENCY IS EASY

Chapter Two

Escaping Your Former State's Taxing Authorities

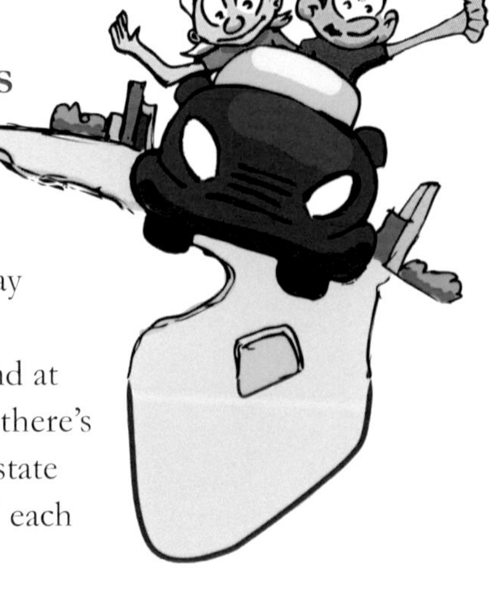

While moderately simple to become a Florida resident, your former state may not so easily release you from its steely grasp. Each state's laws are different, and at floridaestateplanning.com/moreguide there's a summary of all fifty states' income, estate and inheritance taxes and a synopsis of each state's residency requirements.

The common thread throughout most of the states that impose taxes is that even if you declare yourself to be a resident of Florida or any other state, they'll still consider you as their resident for tax purposes if you spend a certain amount of days there, or engage in certain activities.

Earned Income Issues

In almost all instances if you earn income in a state you will be expected to pay income taxes to that state. If, for example, you are a Florida resident but earn income in New York, you are still required to file a state income tax return and pay taxes there. In some states, like New Jersey, you may pay higher taxes as an out-of-state taxpayer as opposed to as an in-state resident.

So if you are still earning income in another state before declaring Florida residency you will want to examine whether that's advisable.

Retirement Source Income

Prior to 1996, some states maintained statutes allowing for "source taxes." These statutes required those who earned pension income in a state to continue paying taxes to that state even though they no longer lived there.

The theory behind the "source tax law" is that the assets accumulated in a qualified tax deferred account are earned while working in that state.

While the taxpayer received an income tax deduction, the state only gets to collect income tax when withdrawals are made. So if the taxpayer moves out of the state then the state should be able to tax the withdrawals to match the corresponding deductions during the taxpayer's working career, no matter the taxpayer's residency at the time of the withdrawals.

Sounds bureaucratic doesn't it? And unfair.

Back in 1989 the Schenectady Gazette reported the plight of a retired woman who earned a pension while working in California. Though the woman moved to Nevada over nine years earlier, she still received a tax bill from the State of California on her pension income. Retirees across the United States faced similar scenarios, thanks to various incarnations of this source tax law.

Congress recognized this unfairness and consequently enacted the Pension Source Tax Act of 1996. This law stipulates that "No State may impose an income tax on any retirement income of an individual who is not a resident or domiciliary of such State." While the Source Tax Law does not restrict how a state defines residency, it prohibits any state from taxing non-residents for pensions, even if earned within that state. If you earn a pension in Vermont, for example, then retire to Florida; Vermont cannot tax your pension income.

Defining Residency

This begs the question. How do states define residency? A quick review of the tax comparisons listed at floridaestateplanning.com/moreguide tells us that Massachusetts, for example, considers anyone who spends more than 183 days a year there a resident no matter where they are registered to vote or obtain a driver's license.

Clients will ask me, "How will my former state even know where I am?

What if I say I was in Florida for more than 180 days over the course of the year?"

In today's day and age, it is easy to determine the time one spends in any location. State departments of revenue will request credit card statements to review where purchases occurred, health insurance records, phone bills, and a host of other information that pinpoints one's location over the course of a year.

Many years ago a client of mine, "Peter" maintained his primary residence in Florida and a secondary residence, a lake cottage, in Minnesota. Peter took all reasonable measures to ensure his Florida residency. He registered to vote here. He registered his cars and got a Florida driver's license. His credit card statements and tax returns all named Florida as his residence. He spent more than half of the year outside of Minnesota.

Peter did, however, spend summers at his lake cottage fishing and enjoying visiting with his grandchildren who lived nearby and often spent the weekends with him. One year, upon returning to the cottage he visited his local supply store where he applied for and purchased a fishing license. Minnesota fishing licenses are slightly more expensive for non-residents than they are for residents. He indicated on the license he was a resident of the state, since he owned a home and paid property taxes there.

Peter died that summer in Minnesota. His family was careful to have his death certificate show that he was a Florida resident. The Minnesota Department of Revenue thought otherwise and imposed a state tax on the entire value of his estate. In supporting their claim, they cited Peter's fishing license application, where he clearly indicated that he was a resident of the State of Minnesota.

Our office denied this was a full admission of primary residency. Peter, we argued, believed that because he owned a residence and paid Minnesota property taxes he would be entitled to the reduced fishing license fee. Long story short, his estate settled for about half of the tax as the costs of litigating would have outweighed the tax assessment. It's a shame though, as the $5 that Peter saved on his fishing license ended up costing his estate several thousand dollars.

Peter's story illustrates how aggressive state taxing authorities may be. We all know that state governments are hurting for revenues, and will therefore look for revenue in any place it can. What better place than to tax residents who no longer vote there?

> DO YOU INTEND TO SPEND THE REQUISITE TIME OUTSIDE OF YOUR FORMER STATE TO QUALIFY FOR NON-RESIDENT STATUS?
>
> DO YOU CONTINUE TO EARN INCOME IN THE STATE?
>
> IS YOUR HEALTH INSURANCE OR OTHER BENEFITS YOU MAY RECEIVE NON-TRANSFERRABLE TO FLORIDA IF YOU SHOULD BECOME A RESIDENT HERE?

Residency Factors to Consider

While the warning is important that doesn't mean that one should give up and succumb to state taxing authorities. When deciding whether to become a Florida resident, several factors should be considered, including:

Furthermore, there may be other questions pertinent to your situation. If you must remain a state resident to retain certain government benefits such as health insurance or Medicaid, and if it would be not likely to match those benefits in Florida, then it may not be a good idea to change domicile.

One reservation that is not pertinent, and which I hear often is this: "I have lived in that state my whole life and I cannot imagine not being a resident of that state!"

To this I raise my eyebrows with a perplexed look. Just because you are no longer a legal resident of a state does not mean you cannot travel within its borders, enjoy the company of family and friends who live there or otherwise feel a close association. It means you no longer wish to make contributions to its taxing authority.

So the real difficulty for those who maintain residences here and in their former home state, becoming a Florida resident is not meeting Florida residency requirements so much as it entails escaping the clutches of your former state's taxing authority.

In the next chapter I review whether your will and/or trust documents drawn in your former home state are invalid once you've become a Florida resident.

KEY TAKEAWAYS

> THOSE WHO MAINTAIN RESIDENCES IN TWO STATES MUST BE COGNIZANT OF THEIR RESIDENCY REQUIREMENTS

> SOME STATES TREAT YOU AS A RESIDENT FOR TAXING PURPOSES EVEN THOUGH YOU'VE DECLARED FLORIDA RESIDENCY

> FEDERAL LAW PROTECTS YOUR QUALIFIED RETIREMENT INCOME FROM BEING TAXED IN YOUR FORMER HOME STATE

> WHILE FLORIDA RESIDENCY SAVES TAXES, THERE MAY BE OTHER REASONS TO REMAIN A RESIDENT OF YOUR "HOME STATE".

Chapter Three

Is Your Northern Will or Trust Still Valid?

A myth I would like to put to bed right away is that a northern will or trust does not become invalid when you become a Florida resident. If the will or trust document is signed properly under the laws of the state in which you are domiciled at the time, moving to Florida does not invalidate the document.

With that said, each state's laws are different. If one doesn't update one's estate plan upon becoming a Florida resident, unintended adverse consequences may arise. When we review the descent and devise rules of Florida homestead below you'll understand how a plan that was just fine as a resident of a different state could create expensive headaches without updating to Florida law.

Updating to Florida Law

So exactly what does it mean to update your estate plan to Florida law? Many recognize that somewhere in their wills and trusts there is a provision that states "The laws of the State of Pennsylvania shall govern this will," (or wherever you may come from).

Linda and Larry arrived in my office wanting only a simple amendment to their Pennsylvania wills. They owned a residence in Pennsylvania that was in Linda's name and a residence on Sanibel in Larry's name. Their bank and brokerage accounts were divided between them, with Linda and Larry each owning about half.

"Our Pennsylvania attorney told us that our documents were fine," Linda began, "and he also told us he is licensed in Florida. So all we want you to do is do a simple amendment changing the state law from Pennsylvania to Florida."

"It's not so simple," I began, "let me show you why we need to do more than that to update your documents to Florida law."

One of my pet peeves, by the way, is the attorney who is licensed in Florida but doesn't practice here – yet speaks with authority about Florida law. While the northern attorney may have passed the Florida Bar, if he rarely practices here it's easy to miss significant issues.

Because your northern attorney may have gained your confidence over the years, you may be predisposed to take her word over mine. After all, you have just briefly met me during our initial consultation where I told you of the various issues that require updating.

As you will see in my trademarked Family Estate & Legacy Program® described more completely in Chapter Ten, we invite your advisors to take part in your planning, including your long-time attorney if you would feel more comfortable with her as a part of the process. We believe that by including those whom you are most comfortable we will arrive together at the best possible plan.

Descent and Devise of Florida Homestead

Returning to the homestead issue as presented in my Linda and Larry illustration – this is the most common problem I see from clients who become new Florida residents. Before I explain what needs to be adjusted in Larry and Linda's estate plan now that they are Florida residents regarding the disposition of the homestead, first allow me to explain why their Pennsylvania attorney divided up their assets, some in Linda's name and others in Larry's.

Recall that when Linda and Larry prepared their Pennsylvania estate plan, their attorney divided up their assets between Linda's name and Larry's name. The reason their assets are divided between them is because at the time they signed the documents, the estate tax laws required spouses to divide their assets to fully consume their combined exemptions against federal estate tax.

Under the law prior to 2011, if one spouse died with all assets in joint name with their surviving spouse, or if he left everything outright to his surviving spouse in a will, then all the couple's combined assets would be included in the surviving spouse's estate for federal estate tax purposes.

In Figure 3-1 we show Larry predeceasing Linda, with all the assets ending up in Linda's name for federal estate tax purposes.

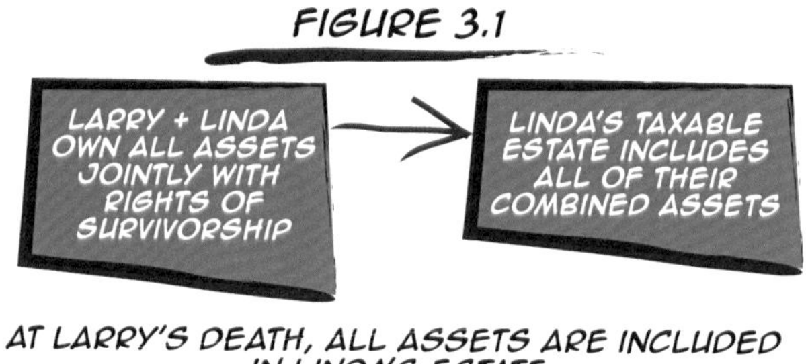

Assume that when Linda and Larry created their Pennsylvania wills, the federal estate tax exemption was only $2 million. They jointly owned both of their residences with rights of survivorship. The Sanibel residence had a fair market value of $1.2 million, and the Pennsylvania residence was worth $1.5 million. Linda and Larry also owned joint bank and brokerage accounts totaling $4 million.

Their combined net worth of $6.7 million would be included and taxed in Linda's estate. Since the exemption at that time was $2 million, the federal estate tax would have approximated at $1.8 million assuming a 38% effective tax rate. In addition, there would also be Pennsylvania estate and/or inheritance taxes due.

The way to combat this problem was to divide Linda and Larry's assets between them. Not only would the division have been necessary, but a "family," "credit shelter," or "bypass trust" (also referred to as an "A/B" trust – these all achieve the same purpose) would have been created inside of their wills. These are known as "testamentary trusts" as they are activated inside of the will upon the decedent's death.

This family trust's purpose is to consume the first decedent spouse's federal estate tax exemption yet preserve the assets for the use and benefit of the surviving spouse. Without embedding a family trust inside of Larry's will in my illustration, the married couple would have lost the opportunity to use Larry's federal estate tax exemption.

In Figure 3-2 you'll see the net result of the Pennsylvania attorney's advice. He had Linda and Larry divide up their assets between them. Recall that the Sanibel home went into Larry's name, and the Pennsylvania residence into Linda's. They also split their bank and brokerage accounts so that individually they each had $2.0 million.

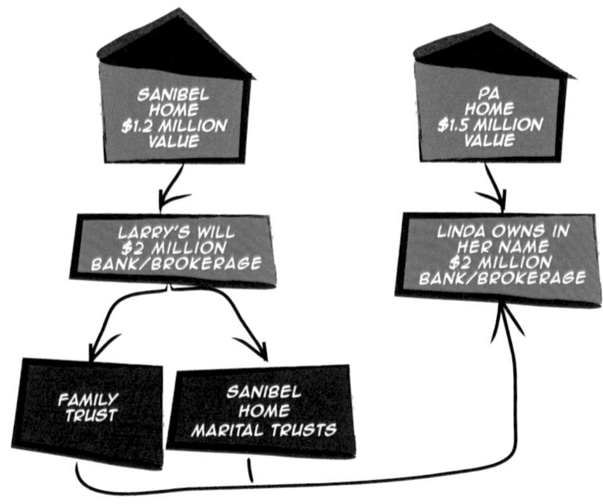

They created and signed wills with a family trust built in. Linda does not legally own the Family Trust created in Larry's estate at Larry's death, but she would still control the trust, and also benefit from it. The Family Trust was "funded" with Larry's assets up to the $2.0 million of federal estate tax exemption he had available at the time of his death.

The excess of Larry's net worth, the $1.2 million Sanibel residence, would be funded into a marital trust for Linda's benefit. Linda would continue to act as the trustee for the trust and was its only beneficiary. So then Linda could continue to live in the Sanibel home as she always had. Marital trusts defer estate tax until the surviving spouse's estate, or as you will learn later in this chapter, could mitigate or even eliminate the estate tax.

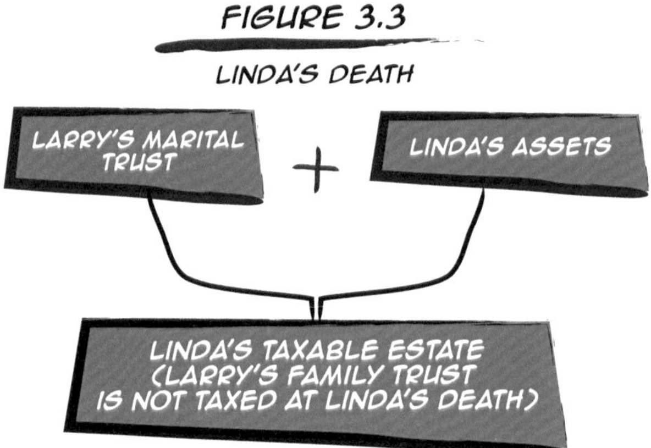

On Linda's death (See Fig. 3-3) her estate now includes the Pennsylvania residence, her bank and brokerage accounts, and the Sanibel residence that is held in Larry's marital trust, where the values of same total $4.7 million. Assuming a 32% effective tax rate, the federal estate tax on Linda's death approximates $860,000. This is a significant decrease from their plight before creating the estate plan – which would have resulted in federal estate tax approximated at $1.8 million – a reduction over $900,000 by dividing their assets and creating estate tax savings trusts inside of their wills!

How Florida Residency Affects the Plan

So what's the legal problem when Linda and Larry became Florida residents?

Nothing changed factually other than the state of residence. Larry still owned the Sanibel residence and half of the bank and brokerage accounts. Linda still owned the Pennsylvania residence and the other half of the bank and brokerage accounts. Larry's will still conveys the Sanibel residence in trust for Linda's benefit when he died first.

And that's the problem.

At Larry's death recall that his will devised their Florida homestead into the "Family Trust" or "Marital Trust". Florida law mandates that when you are married, absent a valid nuptial agreement to the contrary, any devise of the home other than to your spouse is invalid.

While both the Family Trust and Marital Trust inside of Larry's will both dictate that the assets are held exclusively for Linda's benefit for the remainder of her life, the devise of the home is not outright to Linda.

Because of this invalid devise under Florida law the devise of the homestead would no longer be dictated by Larry's will no matter what it says.

Instead, Florida law provides that Linda either receives a life estate in the homestead, or an undivided one-half (½) interest as tenants in common. Who gets the remainder interest if Linda elects the life estate? Who receives the other half interest if she elects that choice? In both instances it is Larry's descendants.

What does this mean? Linda owns the home with Larry's children, no matter what is specified in Larry's will. Larry's children may be Linda's children too, or they may not be if theirs is a blended family.

Larry's children may be minors, or they may be adults. Linda cannot sell the residence without their consent, and must share any sales proceeds with them. If one of Larry's children has creditor problems or is getting a divorce, then that problem may cloud the title to the residence. These are just a few of the legal and tax problems that exist when you have an invalid devise of your home under Florida law.

Generally, no surviving spouse wants to have these complications.

Wills Subject to Probate

Here's another issue with Linda and Larry's estate plan. Many believe that since Linda and Larry had wills their estates will avoid probate. This is false.

Some people believe that if their estate value is less than whatever the federal estate tax exemption is (see the current federal estate tax exemption amount at floridaestateplanning.com/moreguide), then there won't be a probate. That's false too.

Almost any asset subject to disposition by your loved one's will is distributed by the probate process. Understanding what probate means, is crucial to understanding these issues.

The Probate Process

Probate is a legal process under which the deceased's assets are transferred to their beneficiaries. Larry's assets would be probated and then transferred to the testamentary trusts (the Family Trust and Marital Trust). The Last Will is filed with the probate court in the state and county in which the decedent lived at the time of his or her passing. This is known as the "domiciliary estate."

The personal representative (executor) in the will petitions the court for "Letters of Administration" which gives the personal representative the authority to transact business on the decedent's accounts.

It does not matter whether bank and brokerage accounts are held in the same state in which the probate is opened. A bank account in Pennsylvania, for example, is governed by the probate court in Florida.

If, however, the decedent owned real property in his or her individual name in another state, then an "ancillary probate administration" usually must be opened in that state. On Linda's death, for example, since she owns real property in Pennsylvania, her estate would require both a domiciliary administration (since she is a Florida resident) and an ancillary administration in Pennsylvania.

Why is probate necessary? It's not just for attorneys to make fees, as you might be thinking right about now. The probate process "protects" both the beneficiaries of the estate, any potential creditors and of course, the taxing authorities.

Imagine that there was no probate process. Suppose in a codicil to his will your Uncle Ed left you his entire estate. Then again, what if Uncle Ed dies and your cousin brings a copy of his old will into the bank and ask that his accounts be distributed to him pursuant to that older will. How does the bank really know that this is Uncle Ed's Last Will? What if your cousin beat you to the bank, and you didn't realize it? What recourse would you have once the bank distributed to your cousin? The probate process protects against just this scenario and many others.

If you submit a will as the Last Will of Uncle Ed to the court, and someone else submits a codicil to the will to the same court, now we have a centralized system that can ensure Uncle Ed's final wishes are carried out. The personal representative of the will organizes all the assets of the deceased and files an inventory with the court so all interested parties can determine in full light what the estate is worth. They can also question if the inventory is complete or is missing assets.

Florida law provides that creditors have three months from the "notice of publication" date of probate administration to file a valid claim against the estate. There are laws that deal with creditors, how they are to make claims, and how the personal representative may object to a claim. The personal representative has a duty to notify reasonably ascertainable creditors of the administration.

Once all the creditor claims are dispensed with and all tax clearances are obtained, the personal representative submits an accounting statement of the estate to the court. All the income and expenses are listed as are items of capital gain and loss. The personal representative then presents a schedule of proposed distributions pursuant to the terms of the will.

The distributions may be to beneficiaries, or to trustees of testamentary (after death or continuing) trusts established under the terms of the will as in the case of Larry's will noted above. All the beneficiaries have the chance to object to any item listed in these petitions, and can appear before the court. A judge decides if any objection has merit.

Once all the distributions are made, the personal representative petitions to close the estate and be discharged from further obligations as a fiduciary for the estate. Receipts of distributions are filed with the court.

So as you can see, probate is a strictly supervised court (public) process. It is very hard for any "monkey business" to get by a judge.

Cost and Complexity of Probate

So why didn't Linda and Larry's Pennsylvania lawyer use Revocable Living Trusts as opposed to wills? In many northeastern states, the probate process is not as onerous as it is in Florida, and one can accomplish it without hiring an attorney. I've had several Pennsylvania attorneys tell me that probate is not a significant issue for Pennsylvania residents.

Not so in Florida.

While probate is nothing to be feared, if you can minimize a public court process over your assets at the time of your death, the more private and less cumbersome will your administration be. It should also be less expensive. The Florida statutes calculate a reasonable attorney's fee for the ordinary services related to a probate administration. That same fee is reduced by 25% for those same services in a trust administration. A revocable trust therefore can be expected to save significant attorney's fees.

The fact that Larry's will contains an invalid devise and is subject to probate are two important reasons they should update their Pennsylvania estate plan to Florida law. There are many others.

In the next chapter I contrast a will with a revocable living trust.

KEY TAKEAWAYS

- NORTHERN WILLS AND TRUSTS ARE VALID IF PROPERLY SIGNED IN YOUR FORMER STATE OF RESIDENCE;
- EVEN THOUGH YOUR NORTHERN WILL AND/OR TRUST MAY BE VALID DOES NOT MEAN IT WON'T HAVE UNINTENDED AND ADVERSE CONSEQUENCES ONCE YOU BECOME A FLORIDA RESIDENT;
- ASSURANCES BY YOUR NORTHERN ATTORNEY THAT YOUR NORTHERN DOCUMENTS NEED ONLY A MINOR UPDATE TO ACCOMMODATE FLORIDA LAW SHOULD NOT BE TAKEN AS THE GOSPEL UNTIL A QUALIFIED FLORIDA ATTORNEY AGREES;
- FLORIDA HOMESTEAD DESCENT AND DEVISE STATUTES MAY INVALIDATE YOUR CURRENT DOCUMENT'S DISPOSITION AND LEAVE YOUR SURVIVING SPOUSE WITH SOME SIGNIFICANT LEGAL ISSUES; AND
- PROBATE IS A MUCH LENGTHIER, TIME CONSUMING, PUBLIC AND EXPENSIVE PROCESS IN FLORIDA THEN IT IS IN MANY OTHER STATES.

Chapter Four

Will vs. Trust

In the last chapter I alluded to the differences between wills and trusts. In Florida, anyone with any degree of net worth that would otherwise be subject to probate should investigate whether a revocable living trust, sometimes referred to as an "inter vivos" (or lifetime) trust, would be beneficial.

So let's review the differences between a will and a trust. A will, we all know, is a document that states who you want to administer your estate (your personal representative) and how your estate is to be distributed. The will has no other function. The will is a public document, in that after your death it is filed with the probate court. Anyone can look at your will.

Who can view your probate inventory is supposed to be limited to "interested parties" such as beneficiaries and creditors. It is easy to file a claim against the estate to view the inventory. A false claim would be objected to and dismissed, but not before the claimant had the opportunity to review the probate estate inventory.

Keeping Your Estate Private

Most individuals with significant net worth do not want their estates so easily accessible by the public in this age of identity theft and preying on the susceptible. Your spouse and family can be exceptionally vulnerable at the time of your death, so this is not a time when anyone with any degree of wealth would want his affairs made public.

As opposed to many other states, Florida probate is expensive and onerous. I described the probate process and attorney fees in Chapter Three, and how the typical trust administration is less expensive than the typical probate administration.

Some married couples have separate individual trusts while others have joint trusts. Whether a married couple should have a joint trust or have separate individual trusts is a product of several factors, including whether they have different beneficiaries, have wealth they want to preserve for multiple generations, and whether they are in a long term or second marriage.

I say that trusts are private because absent a dispute among beneficiaries, trusts are not filed with any public court or other institution. No one can go down to the courthouse (or log online into court records) to read your trust following your death. Similarly, the trust inventory is not filed with the probate court. The only parties privy to the trust inventory following your death are the beneficiaries and the trustee, and perhaps, the IRS.

You Maintain Control Over Your Trust Assets

When you create a trust, you transfer your assets to the trust. This does not mean you lose control over them. In almost all revocable living trusts, you serve as your own trustee as long as you are able and willing. You handpick your successor trustee. You name whom you want to serve as the party who will manage your investments. Your successor trustee might be your spouse, an adult child, or other close friend or relative. It may also be a bank or trust company.

A "revocable" trust means just that. At any time you can amend, alter or revoke the trust. The assets remain yours for your lifetime; they are just owned by you through your trust. The taxpayer identification number for your trust is your social security number for as long as you are alive. This means that no other income tax returns other than the 1040 are filed during your life.

When you die with a revocable living trust, there is a trust administration process that your trustee is responsible to conduct prior to making distribution of the trust assets. This is not a court-supervised process and is therefore not as time consuming as no one waits for a judge to act or for a court calendar to clear. You can read more about this process in my book, *Legal Matters when a Loved One Dies.*

Your Will Becomes a Safety Net

When you create a revocable living trust, your attorney will also draft a "pour over" will for you. A pour over will acts as a safety net. In order for your trust assets to avoid the probate process, the assets must be transferred into your trust. (See Chapter Ten to review how our unique process, The Family Estate & Legacy Program® directs those transfers.) If any assets somehow didn't get transferred into your trust, the pour over will catches them and puts them in at your death. There would be a probate process on those assets, but not on the others that made it in.

Trusts Support You if You Become Incapacitated

Trusts also shine over wills when you consider how well they work in the event of your incapacity. Assuming you've placed your assets inside of the trust, in the event of your incapacity your successor trustee seamlessly steps in and acts for you. You either resign or are removed as your own trustee, and the person or party you have named in your stead can manage your trust assets.

Contrast this to when you have a will. Your will does not control your assets during your lifetime. So if you become incapacitated, you need to rely on your agent named in a durable power of attorney document, assuming you have one that is valid and up to date.

The problem with relying solely on a durable power of attorney is banks and brokerage firms are wary of liability when powers of attorney are presented. If a bank accepts a power that is revoked, for example, they could be held liable to the account owner for any losses she incurs because of its use. This means that a bank or brokerage firm may spend a considerable amount of time performing due diligence to ensure the power presented is valid. This due diligence takes time. Time may or may not be of the essence should you become incapacitated.

This is not to say that durable power of attorney documents are not useful. They are. That is why we include them as a part of your estate-planning package. Powers of attorney certainly work for assets outside of your trust, which can include annuities, IRA and 401(k) accounts and life insurance, to name a few examples. Relying solely on a durable power of attorney document to take care of your legal and financial affairs in the event of your incapacity is not as preferable as having a revocable living trust in your arsenal, however.

Documents Become Stale

Even if you have Florida documents, estate plans often fall out of date because of changes to the laws or changes to your family or financial circumstance.

In my next chapter I'll review just a few of the changes to the law that have occurred over the last several years, and why those changes merit updates to your plan.

KEY TAKEAWAYS

> WILLS ARE SUBJECT TO PROBATE

> WILLS ARE PUBLIC DOCUMENTS AND SUBJECT YOUR ESTATE INVENTORY TO PRYING EYES;

> TRUSTS ARE PRIVATE DOCUMENTS - THE ASSETS INSIDE OF THE TRUST FOLLOW A SIMPLER, LESS EXPENSIVE TRUST ADMINISTRATION PROCESS;

> TRUSTS SHINE IN THE EVENT OF YOUR INCAPACITY

Chapter Five

Legal Changes Merit Vigilance

We always ask new clients to bring a copy of their existing estate planning documents to our initial meeting. Then we literally have to blow the dust off before reading them after ten, fifteen or even twenty years in a safe deposit box.

"So, do you still want your sister Marie to act as a legal guardian for your children should you both die?" I playfully ask the grey-haired septuagenarians sitting across the conference table from me.

"Our youngest son is 43 years old," the wife says, blushing slightly.

With that revelation, we all have a good chuckle. Nevertheless there are serious reasons to make sure your estate plan remains up to date. In this chapter I will review five recent changes in the laws that merit careful vigilance inside of your estate plan.

Florida Trust Code

The Florida Legislature overhauled the Florida trust code in 2006 and continues to make changes almost annually. Court cases interpreting the statutes also modify the trust and estate laws. Since Florida is home to a large, wealthy, retiree population, our courts hear a variety of cases that may not commonly occur in other states. Florida's laws are therefore cutting edge.

Failure to keep up with those laws may cause unintended consequence to your estate plan. The descent and devise of your homestead is a prime example. While these laws date back to the nineteenth century, they are new and unknown to many Florida residents. In Chapter Three, I outline why those who have become Florida residents should have a qualified Florida attorney review their plan to ensure that there is no "invalid devise" problem.

More recent changes to the Florida trust code will merit consideration when updating your plan. An example of this is the trustee's duty to provide an annual accounting to all trust beneficiaries following the grantor's death. Suppose, for example, Dad had a trust when he died. The trust contains a marital trust for Mom and then distributes to their two daughters at Mom's death. Upon Dad's death, Florida law (like most other state laws) mandates that the trustee must provide annual accountings to Mom and both daughters.

This annual accounting should provide the beginning balance of the trust, income such as interest and dividends earned, capital gains and losses realized, expenses paid, the amount of distributions that Mom took from the trust, the ending balance and any other significant transactions.

Most of our married clients do not want to provide annual accountings to their children during the surviving spouse's lifetime. Florida law provides a mechanism to circumvent this requirement, called a "Designated Representative". So long as your trust meets the statutory requirements, the surviving spouse need not detail her deceased husband's trust's affairs to her children for the rest of her life.

Sometimes it's not the surviving spouse who worries about this annual filing requirement. Occasionally our clients don't want a child who has addiction problems or another beneficiary who may have unreasonable expectations to receive an annual accounting. Again, the proper use of the Florida laws can help the client circumvent this requirement.

There are other issues addressed in the Florida statutes too numerous to detail here. A thorough review of your goals and concerns will bring out which of the Florida trust laws we will use to meet your objectives.

Decoupling of the State Death Tax from the Federal Estate Tax

Before 2005 the federal estate tax laws coincided with the state death tax laws. If your estate paid a state death tax, for example, a corresponding deduction was given against the federal estate tax. There was, in fact, a standard state death tax deduction provided for on the federal return.

Many states (Florida included) had something known as a "pick up" tax, meaning that the amount of that portion of the federal estate tax allocated to the state death tax deduction would be remitted to the state. This pick up tax did not increase the total amount owed; rather the state shared in the amount that otherwise would be paid to the federal government.

That changed in 2005, resulting in what is called "decoupling". The federal estate tax return no longer provided for state death tax deductions.

A list comparing all fifty states' tax laws is available at floridaestateplanning.com/moreguide. You'll find that some states, like Florida, impose no estate or inheritance taxes while other states, like New Jersey, Minnesota and Massachusetts have severe state death taxes. The federal exemption is typically high (check it out at floridaestateplanning.com/moreguide) but in many states the individual death tax exemption is much lower.

New Jersey's state death tax threshold is $675,000, Minnesota's is $1.6 million and Massachusetts's is $1.0 million. What this means is that a taxpayer could have an estate well below the federal exemption, yet still have to pay state death taxes because her estate exceeded these lower amounts.

Most estate plans of married couples are drafted in such a way so that even if their estate value is high enough to warrant a federal or state death tax, it isn't paid until both spouses are deceased. Assume, for example, that Bill and Bonnie are married. Their attorney helped Bill and Bonnie divide their assets between their two trusts so that no matter who died first, their estate tax exemptions would be entirely applied. (This is no longer necessary in many cases, as I'll discuss in the "Portability" section below).

Assume that Bill dies first. Bill's revocable living trust breaks into two "testamentary" trusts upon his death as indicated in the below diagram. The "Family Trust," otherwise known as a "Credit Shelter Trust," is funded with assets up to the amount of his estate tax exemption on the date of his death. Any overage is directed to the "Marital Trust". Both trusts are held for Bonnie for the rest of her lifetime. Bonnie may also be the trustee of the trust, controlling investment and distribution decisions.

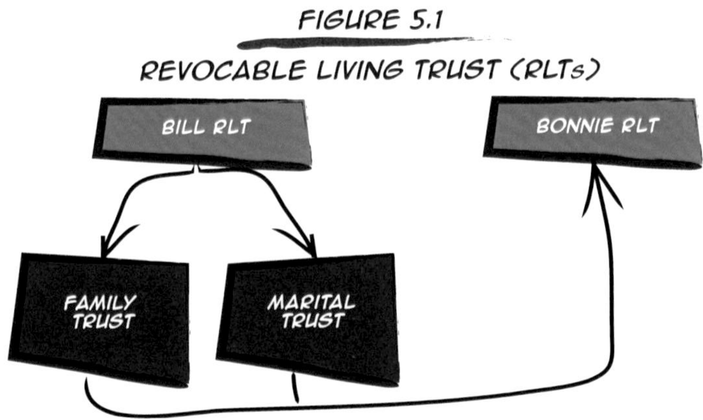

This looks similar to the examples found in Chapter Three, except here we use revocable trust as the primary documents, not wills. By dividing his revocable living trust into a Family Trust and a Marital Trust at his death, Bill's estate uses up his federal estate tax exemption yet pays no tax because the Marital Trust qualifies for the marital deduction. Trusts that qualify for the marital deduction do not pay tax until the surviving spouse dies.

A formula in Bill's trust accomplishes this division. These same formulas are often found in wills where revocable trusts are not used. But here's the rub – if the formula only addresses the federal estate tax exemption and is not drafted in such a way as to consider the lower state death tax exemption, then state death tax could be triggered ***on the first spouse's death!***

This is also true for the formulas found in wills.

That is exactly what occurred in a file that came to me several years ago.

"Bill" and "Bonnie" were New York residents who owned five rental properties in New York State that they rented to third parties. At the time of Bill's death, his estate planning documents drafted before this decoupling law took effect, were not updated.

The formula clause in Bill's trust was based upon the federal exemption, as commonly done. Because New York's state death tax threshold was lower than the federal exemption, his "Family Trust" was over funded for the New York State death tax, triggering a significant tax payment due on Bill's death.

Bonnie had no choice other than to sell one of the rental properties to pay the tax. These rental properties provide Bonnie with her retirement income, so the sale of a property to pay a tax was quite devastating to her.

What's so terrible about this whole mess was that a simple two-sentence addition to the formula clause in Bill's estate plan could have remedied the problem. No New York state death tax would have been paid at Bill's death.

Even after decoupling, many attorneys still use a federal-based formula; particularly attorneys who practice in states that do not impose a state level death tax. This can be a problem for Florida residents who own real estate in states that impose a state level death tax. Without proper drafting, real estate owned in a state that imposes a death tax will trigger the tax if the value of the real estate exceeds the state's exemption amount.

This highlights the urgency of updating your estate planning documents with knowledgeable, qualified estate planning attorneys when you either own real estate in a state that imposes a death tax, or are a resident of such a state.

Portability

Under the pre-2012 federal estate tax law, if a spouse died without using his estate tax exemption, it was lost forever. To illustrate, assume that Thomas and Rita jointly owned all of their assets with rights of survivorship. When Thomas dies, everything he owned is now owned by Rita. Even if Thomas's estate is worth billions, because of the unlimited marital deduction there is no tax on his death. But at Rita's death, their entire net worth would be taxed in her estate. Thomas's exemption was lost because they jointly owned all of their assets with rights of survivorship.

The way to remedy that situation in the pre-2012 law was to divide their assets and implement a "Family Trust" or a "Credit Shelter Trust" (some refer to these as A/B trusts) as I illustrated above in Figure 5.1 of my Bill and Bonnie example.

That all changed in 2012 when "portability" became permanent (or at least as permanent as the federal estate tax law can be). With portability, even if the first decedent spouse didn't set up a testamentary Family Trust to use his exemption, the unused portion can be transferred to his spouse. This is accomplished when the estate files a Federal Estate Tax Return Form 706 and makes an appropriate election on that return.

So if the federal estate tax exemption is $5.45 million at Thomas's death, and he hadn't used any of his exemption during his lifetime and jointly held everything with Rita at his death, his entire unused exemption could be transferred to Rita resulting in her having a $10.90 million exemption at her death.

Failure to Update Could Result in More Capital Gains Tax

If your estate plan predates portability, or if your attorney didn't consider the effects of portability on estates less than the current exemption amount (see that amount at floridaestateplan.com/moreguide), it's possible that your beneficiaries won't enjoy the maximum capital gains tax savings.

If dividing assets between spouses' trusts is no longer necessary to achieve estate tax savings, doing so with standard planning ("Family Trust/Credit Shelter Trust") fails to consider the best way to use the step-up in tax cost basis that our estate assets receive at our passing.

Allow me to explain: assume that I purchased a share of Company A stock on the New York stock exchange for $1/share. My tax cost basis in those shares of stock is therefore $1/share. Over time, the value of that stock increased to $10/share. If I sold the stock during my lifetime at $10/share, then I would realize a $9/share capital gain ($10 selling price minus $1 tax cost basis) and pay taxes on that gain when I filed my annual income tax return.

If instead I died still owning those shares at $10/share, my estate receives a "step-up" in tax cost basis equal to the fair market value as of the date of my death. If my estate and/or my beneficiaries sell the stock the day after my death for $10/share, then they realize no capital gain and pay no capital gains tax.

FIGURE 5.2

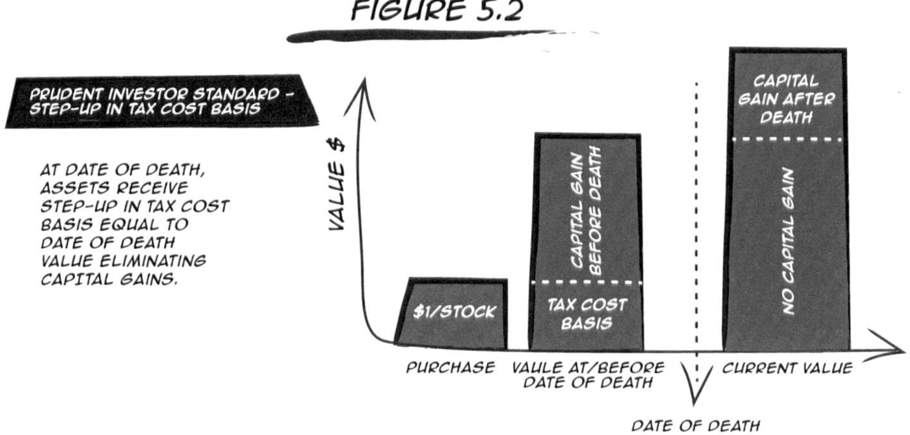

Here's how an estate might pay more tax rather than less. Assume that Thomas has a trust worth $2.5 million at the time of his death, and that Rita has a trust worth $1.5 million. At his death, Thomas's trust becomes a Family Trust that benefits Rita. Rita filed a federal estate tax return on Thomas, even though his estate was not above the filing threshold. She received his unused exemption credit of $2.95 million (let's use a $5.45 exemption minus $2.5 fair value of his estate at his death), so her total exemption is now $8.4 million ($5.45 plus Thomas's unused exemption of $2.95).

Assume further that Rita survives Thomas by 12 years, and in that time frame Thomas's trust has grown from $2.5 million at the time of his death to $3.5 million at the time of Rita's death. During that same time period, Rita's has grown to $3 million.

When Rita dies, her estate benefits from a step-up in tax cost basis to $3 million. If her estate or her beneficiaries were to sell the assets in her trust at $3 million, there would be no capital gains tax paid. Further, Rita's estate is far below her exemption of $8.4 million, so no estate taxes are paid either.

While Thomas's trust enjoyed a step-up in tax cost basis to $2.5 million at his death, there was no corresponding step-up of the Family Trust assets at the time of Rita's death, when under the Portability law his trust could have been designed to do so. Consequently, the $1 million of unrealized appreciation between the time of Thomas's death and Rita's death could have been wiped out.

Thomas's trust, for example, could have included a Marital Trust for the benefit of Rita instead of a Family Trust.

FIGURE 5.3

THOMAS DIES LEAVING EVERYTHING IN TRUST FOR RITA

SINCE THOMAS LEFT ALL OF HIS ASSETS IN MARITAL TRUST FOR RITA, ALL OF THE ASSETS ARE INCLUDED IN HER ESTATE AND ENJOY A STEP-UP IN TAX COST BASIS BOTH AT HIS DEATH AND HERS

While a Marital Trust would not have used Thomas's exemption from federal estate tax, the use of his exemption was unnecessary given this fact pattern. By creating a testamentary trust that qualifies for the marital deduction, Thomas's trust assets receive a step-up in tax cost basis both at his passing and then again at his wife's death. This eliminates the capital gains tax exposure that is generated during that time frame.

My illustrations here are simplified to explain these complex tax issues. The point I make here is how portability turns traditional estate planning methods on their head when one of the considerations is to minimize taxes – both estate taxes and capital gains taxes.

There are many other laws you should be aware of that have changed in the last few years. I've established very clearly why sticking your estate planning documents in a drawer without keeping them up to date could cause adverse consequences.

In the next chapter I'll review what you need to know about updating all of your durable power of attorney, health care surrogate and living will documents.

KEY TAKEAWAYS

> THE TRUST LAWS AND THE TAX LAWS ARE IN A CONSTANT STATE OF CHANGE

> KEEPING UP WITH THESE LAWS CAN HAVE A REAL ECONOMIC EFFECT ON YOUR LOVED ONES

> THERE'S NO FORMULA THAT APPLIES ACROSS THE BOARD - WHAT'S GOOD FOR ONE FAMILY MAY BE ENTIRELY INAPPROPRIATE FOR ANOTHER

> HAVING A QUALIFIED, KNOWLEDGEABLE ATTORNEY WHO KEEPS UP WITH THESE CHANGES IS PARAMOUNT TO YOUR PLAN'S SUCCESS

Chapter Six

Durable Power of Attorneys, Health Care Surrogates, Living Will

Your will and trust are not the only estate planning documents that should be both reviewed and updated. As each state's laws are different for wills and trusts, they are also different for durable power of attorneys, health care surrogates, and living wills. The laws that govern these important documents often change.

Durable Power of Attorney

In 2011 the Florida statute governing powers of attorney substantially changed the way Durable Power of Attorney (DPOA) can be used in Florida.

A DPOA is an important document that everyone should have as a part of his or her estate-planning portfolio. The grantor of a Durable Power of Attorney names someone who can legally act for the grantor in any number of ways. The person who is granted the power to act is known as the "attorney-in-fact" or "agent." For simplicity's sake I will refer to the grantee of the power as the "agent."

The DPOA may allow the agent to write checks to pay bills, sign deeds, complete beneficiary designations, enter into and/or enforce contracts, open accounts, close accounts, and direct investments.

DPOAs cease upon the grantor's death. In other words, once the grantor of the DPOA dies, the document is no longer effective. The "Durable" in the name "Durable Power of Attorney" means that the powers survive the grantor's ***incapacity***. A General Power of Attorney, in contrast, would cease once the grantor becomes incapacitated such as through dementia or Alzheimer's disease. Most estate plans use the DPOA since the thought is that the power holder would normally only act if the grantor of the power couldn't.

Springing Durable Powers of Attorney

Under Florida law prior to the 2011 change, one could name an agent under a DPOA, and then if that agent is unable or unwilling to serve, another agent can be named as an alternate. It might look something like this: "I hereby name my wife Patricia as my Attorney-in-Fact and if Patricia is unable or unwilling to serve then I name my daughter Gina to so serve." This is known as a "springing power". Some of these old springing powers could be grandfathered in under the new statute.

But they're not practical.

Why? Successor DPOAs are very difficult to use from a practical standpoint.

Consider that any bank, financial firm or broker acting under a DPOA will be suspicious of the document from a liability standpoint. Consider the scenario where daughter Gina walks into her father's financial advisor's office holding the DPOA and says "I need to transfer $20,000 out of my father's money market account today."

My financial advisor looks at the DPOA, worried that if it is not authentic he could be liable for following Gina's direction. So he asks Gina, "Why are you using the power? Can I call your dad to see if this is okay?"

"Dad's in the hospital and isn't able to talk. I need to write checks to pay a bunch of his bills and that is why I am here," Gina answers him.

Dad's financial advisor then reads the DPOA – and points to the first line that says his wife Patricia is the first power holder and not Gina.

"It says here that your mother is the first power holder and that you can only act if she can't," he says.

"My mom is out of the country and can't take care of these things now," Gina says.

"I'm sorry," financial advisor says, "I have to be very careful as I may have a lot of liability here if for some reason you aren't supposed to act," he says. "I will give this to my firm's legal department to sort out."

Gina is frustrated and worried that she won't be able to pay her father's bills on time. "How long will this take?" she asks.

"I don't know," the financial advisor replies.

From there the whole thing can become a circus. The attorney for the financial firm may say they need written proof that Patricia can't act, or she is unwilling to act. It can take days if not weeks to resolve.

Concurrent Durable Powers of Attorney

So what's the alternative? What we suggest is that each person you wish to name as your agent under a DPOA have an individual DPOA document that just names them. While there is a possibility that if you have two different parties acting under a DPOA that they conflict with one another, I will tell you anecdotally from personal experience I have seen little (if any) of that in my practice.

With that said, if you name more than one party as a DPOA in separate documents it is wise to tell the individuals you are naming of the fact that each has a separate, concurrent power, and you expect them to work together and to consult one another. Or, if you prefer that one only act when the other couldn't, that would be a verbal arrangement.

Remember that anyone acting as an agent under a DPOA has a fiduciary duty to the grantor of the power. She should only act in the grantor's best interests. If you fear that someone you name won't do that, or won't work in conjunction with another as you would request, then I would say you shouldn't be naming that person in such a powerful document to begin with.

Superpowers Require Initials

Another important point to the new statute is the requirement that certain powers must be initialed to be effective. The banking and financial firm lobbies became concerned that clients weren't truly aware of many provisions buried in multi-page documents. It is not sufficient for your document to state that your agent can do anything you can do.

The powers must be specifically stated, and as said above, certain "superpowers" require the grantor to initial. These superpowers include the power to make gifts from the grantor's assets, the power to create and amend trusts, and the power to create and amend beneficiary designations.

Even those with revocable trusts, however, often own assets outside of the trust such as IRAs and annuities. If the original account owner becomes incompetent you still need a durable power of attorney to take care of those accounts, along with a host of other issues, such as enforcing contractual and legal rights, preparing beneficiary designations, performing tax planning, signing tax returns, and so on.

I hope you don't come away from this chapter believing durable power of attorney documents are not crucial to anyone's estate plan. They are. That's why I'm emphasizing keeping the crucial durable power of attorney document up to date.

Health Care Directives

Besides the durable power of attorney, your complete estate plan includes advance directive documents including the health care surrogate and living will. The health care surrogate names someone to make important health care decisions for you. It allows your surrogate to sign admissions forms to hospitals, rehabilitation and long term care facilities, as well as to interact with your medical professionals including making decisions regarding your care.

Under a Florida law enacted in 2015, your health care surrogate can either decide for you in the event of your incapacity, or along with you when you are competent. Florida's health care surrogate statute also enables you to name a separate surrogate to make mental health care decisions for you.

Living Will

The living will document, sometimes referred to as "the right to die" document, enables you to make end-of-life decisions while you are competent regarding the withholding or withdrawing of life-prolonging procedures so long as you meet the statutory precondition.

Florida's living will law provides that you must be in an "end stage" terminal condition, or in a "persistent vegetative state" with no hope of recovery. This condition must be certified by two physicians and is signed off on by the surrogate named in your living will, who is also your health care surrogate.

Terri Schiavo was a woman central to one of Florida's (and the nation's) most famous living will cases. Terri lived in Dunedin, Florida (near Clearwater). She suffered a massive heart attack in 1990 and was resuscitated only to be left comatose in a persistent vegetative state. She had never signed a living will.

Her husband argued that she would not have wanted to live on in this manner and petitioned to have her feeding tubes removed. Her parents disagreed with the medical diagnosis and went to court to stop her husband's direction. After a seven-year court battle, along with her case being made the subject of state and federal politicians comments, including then President George W. Bush, her tube was removed and she died in 2005.

No one wants the end of his or her life to become the circus that Terri Schiavo's case became. The living will document minimizes that possibility. By signing a document indicating what your direction would be if you met the legal preconditions, you are in charge. You let your loved ones know exactly what you would want in such an unfortunate situation.

Documents Valid in Other States

If you are a resident of Florida then your advance directive documents should comply with Florida law. Sometimes I'm asked by a client, "If I'm at my residence in Massachusetts and end up in a hospital there, wouldn't I need Massachusetts documents?"

The answer to that question is, "No." So long as you have documents compliant with your state of primary residence, then any state where you may end up in the hospital will accept your health care directives.

The Family Estate & Legacy Program® includes a review and an update of all of your advance directive documents at the time we update your estate plan. Moreover, as you can see from this chapter, keeping up with the changes in these laws is as important as the changes that affect your will and trust.

KEY TAKEAWAYS

- STATE LAWS AFFECT YOUR ADVANCE DIRECTIVES SUCH AS YOUR DURABLE POWER OF ATTORNEY, HEALTH CARE SURROGATE AND LIVING WILLS;
- THESE LAWS CHANGE FREQUENTLY, SO IT IS IMPERATIVE TO KEEP THESE IMPORTANT DOCUMENTS UP TO DATE AND COMPLIANT WITH YOUR STATE OF RESIDENCE;
- YOUR ADVANCE DIRECTIVE DOCUMENTS THAT ARE COMPLIANT WITH YOUR STATE OF RESIDENCE ARE ALSO RECOGNIZED IN ALL 50 STATES

Chapter Seven

Protection for Yourself, Your Spouse and Your Beneficiaries

At this point in the book, it is my hope I've convinced you that estate planning should not be a "let's take the old documents out of the safe deposit box to review them every 10 years" proposition, particularly for anyone with any degree of net worth. While working with your legal team to update your plan, I suggest that you also consider adding three key ingredients that your plan may not already have:

- Protection
- Asset Alignment
- Client Care

When I refer to "protection" I separate them into three components – protection for yourself, protection for your spouse, and protection for your beneficiaries such as your children and grandchildren.

"Asset Alignment" speaks to having your assets owned in the right "basket". As you'll learn in Chapter Eight, if you never get around to transferring your assets into your revocable trust, you might as well not have a trust.

"Client Care" refers to keeping your legal documents up to date with the ever-changing estate, trust and tax laws, as well as with your personal and financial situation.

Ensuring that these three elements are functional inside of your estate plan should provide you and your loved ones with comfort and clarity.

In this chapter we examine the element of protection and then discuss Asset Alignment and Client Care in the following chapters.

Protection for Yourself

Many clients mistakenly believe that by creating a revocable living trust, they protect their assets from the claims of divorcing spouses, predators and creditors. This isn't the case. When you transfer assets from your name into your revocable trust, you only change the form of ownership. Because you own the trust, the trust assets are still considered yours, therefore you can change the terms of the trust whenever you want, and you control the disposition of trust assets.

Revocable trusts use your social security number as the tax identification number, so there's no separate income tax return to file as long as you are alive. All the income of the trust appears on your federal Form 1040 just as it always has.

Because assets inside of your trust remain legally yours, the trust does not shield you from liability.

This came to light when a client of my firm accidentally killed a motorcyclist while driving her car. A retiree, she had moved to cut expenses, limiting her automobile insurance coverage to 100/300/50, meaning she had coverage of $100,000 bodily injury liability insurance per person, $300,000 total bodily injury liability insurance per accident, and $50,000 property damage liability per accident.

She unfortunately also dropped her umbrella insurance policy. Umbrella insurance is extra liability insurance that stacks on top of your home, auto and boat coverage. It helps protect you from major claims and lawsuits. In today's litigious age umbrella policies are critical to protect your assets and your future. A $2 million umbrella policy, for example, will provide additional coverage above the limits of your liability policies. Usually you must increase your home, auto, and boat coverage to the maximum limits when purchasing an umbrella policy. For most people, umbrella policies are very affordable.

Our client's insurance wasn't adequate to cover the losses associated with her accident. Much to her and her adult children's surprise, this meant that her other assets, including those assets funded into her revocable trust, were at risk in the negligence lawsuits following the incident. The lesson to be learned is to carry adequate insurance, and even if you are retired it makes sense to carry an umbrella insurance policy.

Disability Protection

While your trust does not offer liability protection, it offers other types of protections for you. A well-drafted trust includes extensive disability provisions. Since most clients serve as their own trustee, the primary danger often relates to cognitive decline.

I can best illustrate this issue by relating another incident we saw in my office not too long ago. I received a call from one of my client's adult children, "Kevin".

"Craig," he said, "I think we have an issue with Dad."

"What's that?" I asked.

"Well, I am down visiting from Michigan," he began, "and when I arrived here yesterday I found a big pile of unopened mail on his kitchen table. There were unopened bank and brokerage statements and bills. I became worried and asked if I could open them up and see what was there."

"I understand your worry," I said. "Maybe we need to get a bill paying service."

"I haven't told you the worst part yet," Kevin said. "When I opened his bank statement I found a $10,000 check written to his housekeeper. He clearly wrote out the whole check – it wasn't written in anyone's hand but his own, and the signature is his. But get this – when I asked him about it – and showed him the copy of the check – he didn't remember it at all."

"Do you think he may have said that to avoid telling you that he really wanted to give her the money? Maybe he's lonely and got attached to her and felt generous."

"No, I really don't. Dad's 93 and I've noticed him slipping. What do you think we ought to do?"

"Well, it's probably time to remove him as his own trustee on the various accounts. You're the successor trustee so we'll begin the Transitional Event Process™ that we've built into his trust. We'll see if your father wants to resign, or if he is resistant we need to take him to a neurologist to get a clear diagnosis on his condition. Meanwhile I'll work to see if we can recover the money he gave the housekeeper."

"Sounds like a plan," Kevin said, somewhat relieved.

Don't take it for granted that your estate plan contains the proper disability protections we used in my client's case. Many trusts contain inadequate provisions to effectively deal with this type of situation.

Defining Disability

First, how is disability defined? Many trusts require a physician to sign a statement that would remove the client from acting as his own trustee. I've had to alter how I draft these provisions because physicians are afraid of liability and won't sign them. So instead I include a provision that requires a physician's diagnosis along with something I refer to as a "disability panel."

This disability panel can include any group of trusted relatives or friends whom the client believes will make informed decisions regarding the client's cognitive decline. If this panel sees that the client could pose financial harm to himself (such as writing $10,000 checks to the housekeeper) then the panel can remove the client so that the next successor trustee steps in.

Sometimes clients will express concern that their disability panel will remove them even though they are still capable to continue on as their own trustee. Anecdotally I'll tell you during my entire career to date (more than 27 years) I can't recall that ever occurring. I can, however recall several instances where the family suspected a problem and waited too long to make the change.

Further, we make it clear in the trust instrument that although the successor trustee is serving, so long as the client is alive he is the primary beneficiary and the trust assets are not to be used for the ultimate beneficiaries until the client has passed away.

There are related issues to consider, such as when a client is financially supporting someone else, or is making gifts to his loved ones for medical or educational expenses. In those instances, it's important to include provisions allowing the successor trustee to continue on as the client would have, even though the client is no longer capable of making those decisions.

Giving Your Successor Trustee Help

Another protection for the client that can and should be drafted into the trust instrument concerns the ability of the successor trustee to enlist help when they need it.

An example of this is when you name your daughter Becky to serve as your successor trustee. Let's say that Becky is married with two children along with working in her career. If you were to suddenly need her to step in and serve as your trustee, Becky may be unprepared to take on a host of important responsibilities including writing your checks, paying bills, ensuring money is moved into the proper accounts to do so, watching over your investments, and filing your tax returns. Becky could most likely use some help. So your trust can allow her to appoint agents, or even name a co-trustee temporarily. While most trusts already provide that the trustee can employ professional agents, I don't see many that allow someone like Becky to hire and fire co-trustees.

The reason Becky may want a co-trustee and not an agent rests with the amount of liability and responsibility she can transfer to another party, such as a bank or financial firm. Sharing the responsibility while remaining control and oversight, along with the ability to hire and fire the co-trustee could be an important power you would want to serve as a protective devise in the event of your incapacity.

Protection for Surviving Spouse

Protecting yourself isn't the only thing that your trust can and should do. Another consideration is to protect the inheritance you leave your surviving spouse. Unlike the trust you create for yourself, it is possible to protect what you leave your spouse against predators, creditors, bad decisions and a variety of other dangers.

One of the most significant decisions you and your spouse will make together is the choice of who your successor trustee will be. Spouses will usually name each other. But is that always the wisest choice?

If your spouse has no experience managing money and you've been a do-it-yourselfer, then you may be setting her up for some big problems. She's likely to search for a financial planner. Who knows whether she ends up with a quality professional who only has her best interests at heart? Wouldn't it be wise to also name a successor co-trustee with her in the document so that is one less decision she would have to make in a time of crisis?

Protecting Inheritance from Remarriage

If that isn't an issue what about protecting your surviving spouse from remarriage troubles? One of the PowerPoint slides in my presentation to prospective clients on this issue shows a picture of J. Howard Marshall and Anna Nicole Smith.

Most people know that story. The Texas multi-millionaire who became infatuated with a lady he met at a Houston strip club, marrying her. We all know how that story played out.

Most of us, even those in second marriage situations, hope that our hard-earned estate will benefit our spouse, but then revert to our children and grandchildren when our spouse dies. With Mr. Marshall, his new wife was considerably younger than his children. Even if he created a marital trust for her lifetime, by the time she would be expected to pass away his children also may not likely be around to enjoy any of their inheritance. As it turns out, Anna Nicole died young. Her drug-addict son was in on her bounty and he died young from an overdose.

Blended Family Issues

While the Marshall/Nicole-Smith example is not all that common, there remain a host of very legitimate issues in blended family situations. When a surviving spouse is not the parent of the deceased's children, tying them together through the use of marital trusts can be problematic.

Who is the trustee of the marital trust going to be? If it is the spouse, what if he does whatever he wants and doesn't let the children know? The spouse has reason to do this as he wears two hats. The first hat is supposed to be as an impartial trustee while the second hat is that of a beneficiary. Those two hats have an inherent conflict of interest.

This doesn't mean you shouldn't name your spouse as your successor trustee. What I'm pointing out is that much thought should go into that process to protect your intent as to how you would like to take care of your surviving spouse, and what specifically you'd like to leave your children and when.

If, for example, you want your spouse to be the highest priority, even if your trust could be exhausted taking care of her for the rest of her life, then it is important that the trust instrument precisely say so. Without language in the trust stipulating what your intent is, it is left to judges and others to decide. Without clear direction, the trustee, whoever that is, has a legal duty to balance the interests both of the lifetime income beneficiary (typically the surviving spouse) against the remainder beneficiaries (those who get what's left after the surviving spouse dies).

Accounting to the Children

There are even other issues you want to protect your spouse from. One example is an accounting requirement to the remainder beneficiaries. Most state laws, including Florida, require the trustee of a testamentary (after death) trust, such as a marital trust, to account to the remainder beneficiaries (often the children) what will happen in the trust each year. Having a will instead of a trust doesn't circumvent this problem as wills also create testamentary trusts for the surviving spouse.

An accounting opens with the balance at the beginning of the year, discloses capital gains and losses realized, income received, distributions made (usually to the surviving spouse), expenses paid, significant transactions and ending balance.

Most of my clients don't want their surviving spouse to live with this requirement. There are legal means to avoid it, but they must be drafted into the will or trust itself. Failure to do so could subject the surviving spouse to financial scrutiny for the rest of his or her life.

These are just a few of the issues that clients should consider to protect their surviving spouse. The facts of your particular situation will reveal what protections and therefore which steps to consider for your spouse.

Protecting Children and Grandchildren

Most wills and trusts I review from my new clients seem, at the surviving spouse's death, to distribute everything outright to the children, unless they are young, in which case the assets are held in trust until the children attain a certain age, such as 30 or 40 before being distributed outright.

I believe that when this happens you've missed a major opportunity in the estate plan. Allow me to explain what I mean.

Protecting Spendthrift Beneficiaries

One of the most common concerns raised by my clients in my conference room centers on whether their children will squander or waste their inheritance. This concern has merit. A Key Private Bank study found that the average inheritance is fully consumed within 17 months. This study included Inherited IRA accounts that could have been stretched out over the lifetime of the beneficiary, but were completely withdrawn, resulting in the early recognition of income (and corresponding payment of income tax) and losing tax-deferred growth.

Protection from Creditors

Protecting from spendthrift tendencies is not the only danger. Proactively protecting your children from creditors could be another issue. When the real estate market crashed in 2007, for example, several of my client's adult children suffered through foreclosure proceedings when they purchased homes at the height of the market and then lost their jobs. When a foreclosure sale occurs on the steps of the courthouse, there are often deficiencies between the amount of the loan outstanding and the sales price. This results in a deficiency judgment against the borrower that accrues interest over time.

Beneficiaries who inherit assets outright when they have an outstanding deficiency judgment (or any other judgment) against them risk losing the inheritance to the judgment creditor. There are all kinds of judgments that could linger for years against your intended beneficiaries, including student loan debt, business deals gone sour, alimony, child support, negligence and malpractice cases just to name a few.

To protect your loved ones' inheritance from these dangers isn't all that difficult, only a change of your mindset from leaving the inheritance outright to leaving it in a continuing trust, otherwise known as a "testamentary", or after-death trust.

Tailor to Specific Needs

Testamentary trust provisions are built inside of your revocable living trust and spring into effect upon your death, or upon the death of the survivor of you and your spouse depending upon the terms. There is no "boilerplate" or "one-size-fits-all" trust. A testamentary trust may be drafted to meet your specific goals and concerns.

If, for example, a spendthrift beneficiary is your concern, then you are likely to name a third-party trustee to manage the investments and consider the distributions to that beneficiary. A third party trustee might be an investment firm, bank or trust company, an attorney, CPA, or other trusted professional, a competent friend or other family member.

Don't Set Family Up for Conflict

Be careful that you do not name a son or daughter to act as a gatekeeper to one (or more) of their siblings' inheritance. That is a recipe for disaster. I explore this and related topics more in depth in my *Selecting Your Trustee* book.

To illustrate, assume that you named your son Bob to act as trustee over his sister Jennifer's trust share. Jennifer asks Bob "I need $40,000."

Bob asks, "Why do you need this money?"

"What's it your business?" Jennifer replies.

"Because Mom and Dad selected me as your trustee and I need to know as I have a duty to protect your inheritance from you spending it away."

"I just need it, okay?" Jennifer says in an agitated voice.

"Well then, no, I'm not distributing it to you!" Bob says.

You can see how these situations can put a strain on the relationship. Don't do it to your kids.

Liberal or Conservative Distribution Provisions

When you direct your attorney to draft these trusts you leave behind for your children and grandchildren, you'll want to discuss how tight the purse strings might be. You can direct, for example, that the trust annually earned income (the interest and dividends), may be a required distribution to the spendthrift beneficiary, but it doesn't have to be. The testamentary trust could be written to allow for discretionary distributions, meaning that the beneficiary must request a distribution and justify the reason for it.

You can have the testamentary trust written to direct the trustee to be liberal with distributions or more tight-fisted. In one situation I had a client who wanted the inheritance to primarily benefit her daughter's retirement years. She therefore had me draft the testamentary trust to only distribute for educational purposes, or for health or support emergencies until her daughter attains age 65. Until that time any extraordinary distribution requests had to be fully justified, and the daughter had to show that she had no other income or assets of her own to satisfy the request. Once the daughter attains age 65, however, the provisions of the trust loosen, allowing the trustee to even make distributions for travel, clothing and other enjoyable pursuits.

More Reasons for Testamentary Trusts

Continuing testamentary trusts are even a great idea for those beneficiaries who do not need a gatekeeper, and who may be superb at managing their own money. No one knows what the future brings. Divorce[1], bad business deals, a malpractice case or a host of other dangers could threaten a child's inheritance. Further, for those über-successful beneficiaries, outright inheritances could only add to existing estate tax issues. Leaving your daughter, the neurosurgeon your wealth might only create additional estate taxes when she dies.

How about the circumstance where you leave wealth to your son, but upon his death he leaves everything he owns to his wife who later remarries? Here the family wealth you have accumulated may not end up

1 Note: Recent case law subjects trust distributions to alimony and child support claims. Trustees may be able to frustrate claimants by accumulating income inside of the trust. These are issues that should be thoroughly discussed with estate planning counsel during the planning stage.

with your grandchildren, rather it could all end up benefitting a family tree you don't even know.

In all of these instances, building a continuing testamentary trust for your beneficiaries will serve to protect the inheritance from these dangers. Instead of naming a third-party trustee gatekeeper, however, you can name the beneficiary as his own trustee. So long as discretionary distributions are limited to provide for "health, education, maintenance, and support," even if the beneficiary controls the investment and distribution provisions, the assets should remain better protected and outside of her estate for federal estate tax purposes.

Separate Shares vs. Pooled

When you build a testamentary trust for your beneficiaries, you should direct your attorney to draft a separate trust share for each beneficiary as opposed to having a pooled trust for all. Your beneficiaries are likely to have separate goals, concerns, assets, risk tolerance, need for income and so on. Upon your death, or the death of the survivor of you and your spouse, the assets will be divided proportionately into the separate trust shares, with each being governed separately from that point forward.

Opportunity Lost

Some clients say "I don't want to go through the hassle of creating a testamentary trust inside of my trust and having my children deal with those complexities. If they want a trust, they can create one like I am right now and put their assets into that trust." Allow me to address both points.

First, while each testamentary trust will have its own separate tax identification number and therefore need to file a separate tax return, governing the trust shouldn't be all that difficult. Your attorney can provide the initial instructions, with your CPA or tax return preparer doing their job annually. Trust formalities are important, but rarely pose considerable problems.

Second, your children can't easily create protected trusts for themselves as you can for them. That ability, for the most part, dies with you. If you haven't created protected trusts inside of your own estate plan, then your family will have lost out on that opportunity. Recall a few pages ago where I informed that your revocable trust offers no protections for yourself. The same holds true when your children create their own revocable trust.

Giving Children Power to Appoint

Finally, clients sometimes object to testamentary trusts as "reaching out from the grave." While a valid concern, there are provisions you can include which mitigate that entirely. You can give your children and grandchildren (and any other beneficiary) a "power of appointment" over their trust share at their death. What this means is that the current beneficiary can alter the default beneficiaries you name for each trust share (normally down the generational line).

An example of this is where you leave assets in trust for your son, Bob. On Bob's death the assets are to be held and distributed to or for the benefit of Bob's children, Cindy and Dan, who become the "default beneficiaries". If nothing else happens, when Bob dies the trust share splits in two for Cindy and Dan.

You choose, however, to leave Bob a power of appointment so he can leave amounts to his spouse, Bonnie, or alter the proportions or amounts he leaves to his descendants, or he can even leave the entire amount to charity. Bob can exercise this power of appointment inside of his will or trust.

So what have you done when you left amounts in a testamentary trust for your children naming each child as the own trustee for his or her own share with a power of appointment to each child at their death? You have given your child the ability to control both the investment and distribution decisions related to his own inheritance along with the ability to also direct the inheritance upon his death. Sounds like an outright distribution doesn't it? In effect, it is not that far off from an outright distribution, but it can provide the protections we reviewed here together.

> REVOCABLE TRUSTS WON'T PROTECT YOU FROM YOUR OWN LIABILITIES. YOU SHOULD ENSURE THAT YOU HAVE ADEQUATE INSURANCE, INCLUDING UMBRELLA POLICIES

> REVOCABLE TRUSTS CAN, HOWEVER, PROVIDE VALUABLE PROTECTIONS IN THE EVENT OF YOUR DISABILITY LEAVING YOU UNABLE TO MANAGE YOUR OWN FINANCIAL AFFAIRS

> YOUR TRUST CAN ALSO BE BUILT TO PROTECT YOUR LOVED ONES SUCH AS YOUR SPOUSE, CHILDREN AND GRANDCHILDREN. THIS IS DONE THROUGH TESTAMENTARY TRUSTS BUILT INSIDE OF YOUR TRUST THAT SPRING INTO EFFECT AT YOUR DEATH;

> THE OPPORTUNITY TO PROTECT YOUR LOVED ONES IS LOST IF YOU DON'T HAVE THOSE PROVISIONS INSIDE OF YOUR OWN DOCUMENTS;

> THERE IS NO "ONE SIZE FITS ALL" PROVISION THAT WILL WORK. THE BEST TRUSTS ARE DRAFTED AFTER CAREFULLY CONSIDERING EACH FAMILY'S CIRCUMSTANCES

Chapter Eight

Asset Alignment

One of the most overlooked assets of estate planning, and in particular with trust planning, is the transfer of the assets to the trust. This can be best illustrated with a true story that occurred in my office just a few years ago when a very nice couple visited me having moved to Florida from Wisconsin. Their Wisconsin attorney, also licensed in Florida, had just completed a revision of their revocable trusts, durable powers of attorney, health care surrogates, living wills and related a pour over will.

They wanted me to represent them since they had become permanent Florida residents. However, they were quick to say they had the utmost of confidence in their Wisconsin attorney who they assured me had taken the necessary steps to update their documents to Florida law. This couple simply wanted to meet with me towards obtaining my help in the future should something happen to either of them.

"Normally I would review your documents and your assets to ensure that your plan is up to date and congruent with your intent now that you live here," I said.

"No thank you. We'll call you when we need you," the husband replied.

That was the last I heard until recently when the wife called me to tell me of her husband's passing. I asked her to provide me current deeds and financial statements so we could implement the testamentary trusts found within their revocable trusts.

That's when we discovered that nothing was ever transferred into either her trust or his trust. "The assets in your husband's name alone will be subject to a probate proceeding in order to get them into the trust for you," I advised.

"But we were told that our trust avoids the probate process," she said.

"It does. That's only when the accounts and properties are titled into the trust name," I continued. "Here, there are accounts in your husband's name. So his pour-over-will catches those assets and deposits them into his revocable trust, but only through a probate process does that occur."

Needless to say, the wife was very aggravated with all the obstacles that appeared before her during a most difficult time – after losing her husband. All of these problems could have been avoided with a review of the trust and the assets and corresponding action taken before anything happened to the husband.

Instruction Sheets Without Follow Up

While you might be thinking that the Wisconsin attorney could have done more, one doesn't know the extent and scope of his representation. Perhaps he wasn't engaged to also transfer the assets to the trusts he created. There are attorneys who simply hand the client an instruction sheet how to transfer their assets to the trust with no further instruction or follow up.

In fact, my firm used to only hand out an instruction sheet. Clients would tell us they will make the transfers themselves, or rather rely on their financial advisor to so assist. They didn't want to pay us to complete this important step.

As you will see in Chapter Ten, The Family Estate & Legacy Program® includes a specific step transferring your assets into your trust. We do it for you. The reason we insist on accomplishing this most important task is because of our experience with clients who try to do it on their own. When we left it up to the clients by furnishing detailed instruction sheets, we found that one of three things happened: the transfer of the assets didn't get completed; it got completed but incorrectly; or it was only halfway completed.

Assets that Should Be Transferred to the Trust

What types of assets need to be transferred into your trust? Your banking accounts, investment accounts, residences and properties, business interests, including closely held business and partnership interests, and titles to vehicles and boats, except that two personal automobiles are exempt from probate in Florida.

As I pointed out with the Wisconsin couple, when the assets aren't properly transferred, adverse consequences can result.

Beneficiary Designations Important

It's not just the transfer of the assets that may be at issue. Some clients own significant IRA, 401(k) and pension accounts, and some also own annuities. Those accounts name a beneficiary which on its face appears to be easy to accomplish. Your will and revocable living trust rarely govern those accounts, but as clients accumulate more and more of their net worth inside of those types of accounts, the estate planning behind them, including preservation of the assets and income tax planning, becomes vitally important.

Estate and income tax planning with annuities and retirement account assets is beyond the intended scope of this book since I will publish another book on that topic. However, keep in mind that "Asset Alignment" may also include completing your beneficiary designations so they fit hand-in-glove with your entire estate plan.

Which Trust Should Receive the Assets?

One issue related to the transfer of the assets is into which trust do you transfer? Some estate plans between married couples forces a choice between transferring the assets into husband's trust, wife's trust and splitting them into proportions of each.

Now that the estate tax rules include "portability" provisions, allowing for unused estate tax exemptions to be transferred from the deceased spouse to the surviving spouse, how to split the assets between a married couples' revocable trusts isn't as consequential as it once was for estate tax purposes.

That doesn't mean that determining which trust to fund the assets into is without consequence. The death of the grantor of a trust results in a step-up in tax cost basis, meaning that the fair market value at the date of death determines the new cost basis for capital gains.

Assume, for example that David bought Coca Cola stock in a regular investment account (as opposed to an IRA or 401(k) account) at $1/share. Assume further that the current price of Coca Cola stock is $10/share. If David sells the stock, he recognizes a $9/share capital gain ($10 sales price less $1 tax cost basis). If David instead died owning the stock whose price on the date of death was $10/share, and the stock was bequeathed in trust to his wife, Rachel, then she inherits the stock at $10/share. If she subsequently sells the stock for $10/share, then she recognizes no capital gain.

Which trust the assets are funded into may have income tax consequences as described above, and there still could be other kinds of issues. Consider, for example, a situation where husband and wife are in a second marriage with children from prior marriages whom they wish to include inside of their estate plan. Therefore, husband's trust and wife's trust contain different beneficiaries. When this is the case, which assets are funded into what trust will have real economic effect to the beneficiaries.

Spousal Elective Share Issues

Yet another Asset Alignment issue relates to spousal elective shares. Most states, including Florida, impose laws that require spouses to leave one another a certain percentage of their estate depending upon a variety of factors. Failure to leave your surviving spouse the minimum required amount could cause the surviving spouse to consider the election to take their minimum lawful share instead of what the estate plan otherwise provided to him or her.

The elective share law may be circumvented with a valid nuptial agreement, but absent such an agreement, the aligning of the assets into the different trusts may have broad ramifications if there is a possibility that either spouse's estate plan could violate the statute.

Finally, there could be trusts other than revocable living trusts involved. If a client institutes an irrevocable life insurance trust (ILIT) as part of her estate plan, then it would be important to change the ownership and beneficiary designations of the polices intended for that trust. Determining which assets go to what trust would have broad ramifications in instances such as this.

We Fund Your Trust for You

As you can see, Asset Alignment is an important element to estate planning, and this is why The Family Estate & Legacy Program® includes a Asset Alignment module. It doesn't end there. How many of us will have the same specific bank accounts, investment accounts, real properties, and other assets today we had five years ago? How do we ensure that our newly acquired assets are properly funded into our trusts?

Not only does your personal financial situation change, but the trust laws and the tax laws also change constantly. Review and change whom you selected to serve as your disability trustee or your death trustee. Perhaps you have new children or grandchildren you want to include in your estate plan since you signed your documents.

The list goes on. Sticking your estate plan in a drawer to gather dust year after year begs for problems. How do you keep up with the changes you not only know of, but those that you don't?

We'll address that in the next chapter.

> YOUR ESTATE WON'T AVOID PROBATE IF YOUR ASSETS AREN'T PROPERLY FUNDED INTO YOUR TRUSTS;

> ATTORNEYS WHO GIVE YOU A ASSET ALIGNMENT INSTRUCTION SHEET AREN'T REALLY COMPLETING YOUR ESTATE PLAN;

> IT'S NOT JUST ABOUT TRANSFERRING THE ASSETS, IT'S ALSO ABOUT WHICH ASSETS GO WHERE;

> IRA, 401(K) AND ANNUITY BENEFICIARY DESIGNATIONS SHOULD FIT HAND IN GLOVE WITH YOUR ESTATE PLAN;

> THE FAMILY ESTATE & LEGACY PROGRAM© INCLUDES AN ASSET ALIGNMENT STEP TO ENSURE THAT YOUR PLAN IS COMPLETE

Chapter Nine

Client Care

You can't avoid rapid change in today's world. Those little silicon chips that appear in everything from our automobiles, to our Smartphones to our home thermostats have dramatically changed how we live, mostly for the better. If you consider what your life looked like a mere five years ago and what it looks like today, chances are you find it amazing how different your personal life is today than it was then.

In Chapter Five we reviewed several legal and tax changes that merit vigilance to keep your estate plan up to date. But your personal situation changes too, doesn't it? Residences are bought and sold, investment and retirement accounts are opened and sometimes moved from one firm to another. Children grow up and grandchildren are born.

All of these changes affect your estate plan. Yet, how long has it been since you've dusted off those documents to take a look with a qualified professional? Two years? Five? Ten? Twenty?!

Don't do that!

Especially if you've just moved to Florida, now is the time to take a fresh look at your estate planning documents. The estate, trust, durable power of attorney, health care surrogate and living will laws have all undergone significant change in recent years. Failure to keep up with those changes could cause significant, costly headaches for you and your loved ones.

Do you remember whom you've named as your personal representative in your will or as successor trustee in your trust? If you've named a bank, brokerage or financial institution, are you still happy with that decision? Does that institution still exist or has a national firm with whom you no longer have any accounts swallowed it?

Alice's Story

A few years ago I had a client, "Alice" who had been with her stockbroker through three financial firm changes. She didn't really care which firm he worked at because she had great confidence in his abilities. And he did a fine job for her.

It was fortunate that Alice came in to my office. As a part of our plan review, we asked her to bring copies of her brokerage accounts. As it turns out, in the haste to move with her advisor from the old firm to the new, his assistant filled out all the paperwork placing the accounts in Alice's name individually, as opposed to as trustee for her revocable trust. They had unfunded her trust. If Alice had died those accounts would have had to go through the probate process.

We also found that while Alice's IRA moved to her advisor's new firm, she hadn't completed new beneficiary forms. Consequently, under the standard custodial agreement governing the account, the default beneficiary was Alice's estate. While Alice's children were the beneficiaries of Alice's estate plan, the result would have been disastrous.

When an estate is named as the beneficiary to an IRA, all the income is recognized in the year following the account holder's death, as opposed to the beneficiaries being able to stretch out the distributions over the course of their lifetimes, deferring the recognition of taxable income and achieving continued tax deferred growth. Since Alice's IRA was over $500,000, more than 40% would have been lost to income taxes alone, not to mention the opportunity cost of no tax deferred growth over her children's lifetimes.

We worked with Alice's financial advisor to properly fund her regular investment account into her revocable trust. Alice completed forms naming Alice's children as the proper beneficiaries to her IRA. Disaster averted.

Ronald's Story

Another client, "Ronald" had a similar situation. He created his trust after his wife's death while a resident of Michigan. He owned two residences, one in Florida and the other in Michigan and a parcel of vacant property in Illinois. When Ronald originally created the trust his attorney transferred the residences into that trust, but not the vacant property.

Eight years after moving to Florida, Ronald decided to update his estate plan to Florida law. That was a good thing since he had remarried without a nuptial agreement. Ronald and his new wife, "Marie" agreed that if he predeceased her then she would move out of their Florida residence so that his kids could take it over.

In the interim, however, Ronald homesteaded his Florida residence. I explained to Ronald under the Florida homestead laws, Marie would have either a life estate interest or a one-half interest as tenants in common if she survived him, even though they had a verbal understanding otherwise. I explained that Florida law imposes the descent and devise of the homestead in a certain manner unless the married couple signs a valid nuptial agreement indicating otherwise.

Further, Marie would have had a spousal elective share up to one-half of Ronald's estate and trust assets if she had survived him. Marie would have had to make an affirmative claim to receive this spousal share, so that may or may not have been likely.

I posed these questions to Ronald, however. "If Marie were incompetent at the time of your death, and if she named her son Tim as her durable power of attorney, wouldn't Tim have an affirmative duty as her fiduciary to make a claim against your estate for the spousal elective share absent a written direction or nuptial agreement otherwise? Further, isn't it in

Tim's best interest to make such a claim against your estate since he is the beneficiary of his mother's estate that would therefore benefit from receiving up to one-half of your estate's assets?"

Then Ronald sold his Michigan residence four years later and bought a smaller townhouse. His title agent deeded the townhouse into Ronald's name individually rather into his trust. Since Ronald now had assets in three different states in his name individually, there would have been three probate estates opened, including the domiciliary estate in Florida, one for the townhome in Michigan and one for the vacant parcel in Illinois.

With Marie's cooperation, these were all rectifiable problems, which were all taken care of during the update to Ronald's estate plan.

More than ever, you can now see how regular maintenance of your estate plan is vitally important. The Family Estate & Legacy Program® has a Client Care program included, as I will describe in the next chapter.

KEY TAKEAWAYS

- STICKING AN ESTATE PLAN IN A DRAWER FOR YEARS INVITES PROBLEMS;
- LAWS CHANGE, YOUR PERSONAL SITUATION CHANGES. YOUR ESTATE PLAN NEEDS TO KEEP UP WITH THESE CHANGES;
- MOVING TO FLORIDA REQUIRES AN UPDATE TO YOUR PLAN

Chapter Ten

The Family Estate & Legacy Program

We've covered a lot of ground throughout these pages. You've learned why it is important to view your estate plan as an ongoing project as opposed to a once-a-decade (or less) exercise. We've explored how a good estate plan may not only provide protection, comfort and clarity for your spouse, children, grandchildren, and other loved ones, but can also save you money, taxes and afford you important protections during your lifetime.

You've seen how a perfectly fine estate plan will become troublesome without updating to the laws of your new home state, and why Florida is one of the best states in the nation to make your new home. We've reviewed how escaping your former home state's tax authority is as important as declaring your Florida residency, and at floridaestateplanning.com/moreguide you'll find a complete synopsis for each of the 50 states' income, gift, estate and residency requirements.

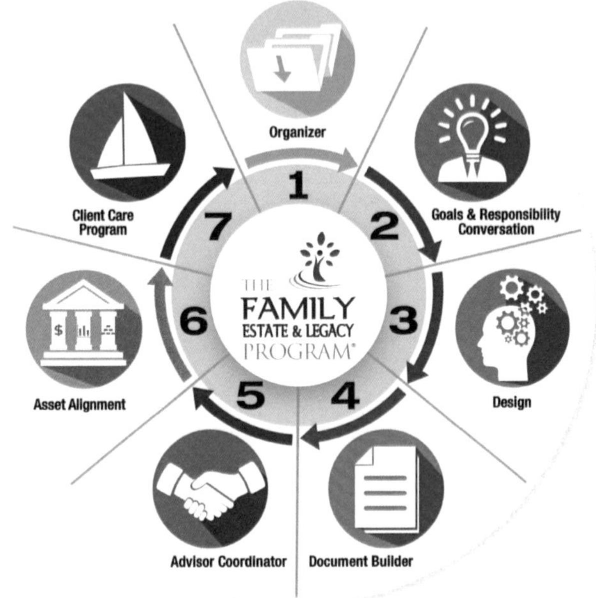

So how do you go about choosing an attorney and a law firm that will navigate these difficult legal, tax and financial waters? To assist you with this important choice, I've created a unique, trademarked process entitled The Family Estate & Legacy Program®. This is a seven-step process that takes you from where you are today to where you need to be for now and into the future.

Organizer

Organizer
1

The first step is our Client Intake Process including our Client Organizer. You may already be familiar with tax organizers that CPAs send out prior to filing your annual Form 1040 Federal Income Tax Return. Our Client Organizer is similar, except it is geared to gather the information necessary for you to make informed decisions relative to your estate plan. For us, as your legal team, the organizer serves to provide us relevant information to maximize your results.

Completing a personal balance sheet is an important element of our organizer. Some new clients push back at this requirement, wondering why we need this information to plan your estate. Realize that a good estate plan is fashioned to the family situation and the type and value of assets they own. An estate plan for someone whose IRA is a larger portion of their net worth, for example, will look very different than an estate plan for a client who may have commercial real estate, which will look different than one in which a family business makes up a large portion of the net worth. The type of assets and their relative values determines the legal strategies that may or may not work for you and your family.

The attorneys and legal teams working under The Family Estate & Legacy Program® understand that spending valuable meeting time gathering information isn't the best use of time. When the Client Organizer is instead completed ahead of the initial meeting, the attorney and his client are likely to have a more productive initial consultation.

We ask that your completed Client Organizer be returned to our office along with a copy of your current wills and/or trusts at least three business days prior to the initial consultation.

Goals & Responsibility Conversation

We start our initial consultation with a conversation eliciting your goals and concerns. Why are you updating your documents? Did you recently move to Florida? Has your family or financial condition changed? Did you read about tax laws that may affect your family? Are you concerned that one of your children's spouses may have their eyes on your child's future inheritance?

Goals & Responsibility Conversation

2

What is it that prompted sitting down with us? We want to hear the answer to that question.

That's because we realize how important it is to listen to your goals and concerns before launching into a discussion as to the advantages of revocable trusts or what provisions you might consider for your will.

It's refreshing to be heard, and to voice the concerns you may have about your estate plan. Once those goals and concerns are thoroughly discussed, your legal team is ready to identify legal and tax opportunities available to you and your family.

A knowledgeable professional will break down the many moving parts that go into a first class estate plan, and explain your choices in simple, easy to understand language. One of the most significant issues that many attorneys don't spend enough time on is specifically who will act in what capacity inside of your estate plan.

In your revocable living trust, for example, you are normally your own trustee until you are no longer capable of serving. So then who should act? Your spouse, perhaps? Is he or she equipped to manage your investments, run the family business or conduct your affairs as you have throughout your lifetime? If not, how should the legal document be drafted to provide him or her all the help needed? Many are wary of banks and trust companies, for example. Be reassured there are ways to accomplish these goals without your beneficiaries having to plead to some corporate institution for a distribution.

How are you going to protect yourself during a period of incapacity? Think about those crucial issues to your welfare, who your successor trustee will be, who will hold your durable power of attorney, and who will be making health care decisions for you. Moreover, what powers do you wish to confer on those you name, and what restrictions will be important?

When you leave amounts to your children, other considerations come to the forefront, depending upon their age, financial savvy, marital status and a host of other factors. Too frequently do attorneys gloss over these issues. In The Family Estate & Legacy Program® we take the time to explore all the possibilities, many of which you may not have previously considered.

In fact, another book on this very subject – Selecting Your Successor Trustee is a part of The Family Legacy Series® used to explore this important topic in depth.

Design

Design

3

Based upon your Client Organizer and the results from our Goals and Responsibility Conversation, we design your estate plan together. We will work together to design a will or trust package that meets your needs, given your family and financial situation, and your goals and concerns. There is no such thing as a "one-size-fits-all" estate plan. The Design element will consider the types of assets you own, how you own them, and the relative tax consequences of your holdings in creating your individualized plan.

Typically, your plan will include a revocable living trust, pour over will, durable powers of attorney, health care surrogate, living will, pre-need guardian and a host of other ancillary documents necessary to effectuate a solid foundation.

For those clients who wish to protect large IRA balances for their loved ones, a Retirement Plan Legacy Trust may also figure into the mix.

While many clients may all have these documents, the contents of each document will be specific to you and your loved one's needs. Married clients may have a variety of marital/credit shelter trusts depending upon their goals and the relative values of their estate. Clients who leave amounts to their children and grandchildren may have continuing trusts to protect the inheritance they leave their loved ones.

All of those marital, credit-shelter, and continuing trusts will have different provisions depending upon the client's goals and concerns. Some distribution provisions may be drafted more liberally, allowing distributions for most any purpose while others may be drafted to be conservative towards protecting a spendthrift beneficiary, or other issues.

Upon zeroing in on a plan, a fixed fee quote is provided. There is no need to worry about how many hours you are spending with the attorney and legal team. The goal of The Family Estate & Legacy Program® is to provide you comfort and clarity. If you feel that every phone call, every email, and every other contact with the firm will result in a higher fee, you may be unwilling to ask all of your questions.

It's important to us you feel you have adequate time to consider your options during this estate planning process.

Once you sign the Service Agreement, we are on to the next stage.

Document Builder

We build all of your documents and send you a written summary and flowchart. The summary and flow chart gives you an easy-to-read, quick reference of your plan. If you want the actual trust drafts, we will forward those to you, but prefer that we meet with you to review them.

Our experience is that when we forward the trust drafts themselves (as opposed to the summary and flow chart), our clients feel they must first read and understand the entire documents before they visit with the attorney again. While we strive to write documents that can be easily understood, there are legal and tax concepts that require us to use language found in the statute books or in the tax law that aren't intuitive for those not well versed in these laws.

That's why we want to take the time to review the actual documents with you. And if it takes more than one review session, we'll do that.

Once you see the design in black and white, you can change certain details. That is why the review sessions are so valuable.

Once your documents receive your approval, we'll proceed towards signing. Once signed, your documents will be scanned and coded into our system, and organized into a binder complete with tabs, the summaries and flowcharts.

But we're not done yet.

Advisor Coordinator

We realize that you may have a trusted attorney from your former hometown, a CPA, and maybe a financial advisor that you would like included in this process. We're happy to include anyone you want. If they are local, they can attend our conferences. If not, or if it is otherwise more convenient, we can conference call them into our conferences.

Remember our most ultimate goal is to provide you comfort and clarity. One giant obstacle to this goal is when a client is receiving conflicting advice. This problem is eliminated when those individuals that you trust are involved in your estate planning process, taking part at every opportunity. We value their input.

For those clients in transition that are looking for a trusted CPA or financial professional, we can recommend trusted and reliable firms to you. Since we've been practicing in our communities for decades, we know those who may serve you well.

Asset Alignment Process

Aligning (or "funding") your assets into your revocable trust is time consuming, tedious, and fraught with technicalities. It's natural for clients to procrastinate funding their trusts, but assets that aren't properly funded won't avoid the public probate process. So we build into The Family Estate & Legacy Program® a Asset Alignment Process that takes care of these details.

Asset Alignment

6

Unlike many firms who hand you a sheet of instructions how to transfer (or "fund") your assets into your revocable trust, we do it for you. Our team includes dedicated Asset Alignment assistants who are well versed in the intricacies of each different financial firm's requirements. They work with you to ensure that everything is in the right "basket" so your estate plan runs smooth.

This is another way that our unique process provides you confidence, comfort and clarity.

Client Care Program

One feature of The Family Estate & Legacy Program® of which we're proudest is our Client Care Program. This unique feature is built to provide you a cost effective way to ensure that your documents do not fall out of date with the ever changing legal, tax and financial world.

Many clients stick their estate plans in a drawer for years, if not decades. This often leads to disaster when the client becomes sick or dies. We know that you don't want to visit with your estate-planning attorney every year, so we created a way for us to come to you.

The Client Care Program works to ensure that your plan keeps up with the changes to your family and financial situation. When you open a new account or acquire a new asset, our team will work with you to ensure that it's titled correctly and fits into your plan.

Near the end of each calendar year, you'll receive a written review of your estate plan. We'll advise as to changes in the trust and tax laws, and if such a law affects your plan, Client Care includes the update. Your estate plan is all about you so the year-end review will provide you the opportunity to tell us about any changes to your family or financial condition that may also affect your planning.

Epilogue

Getting Started

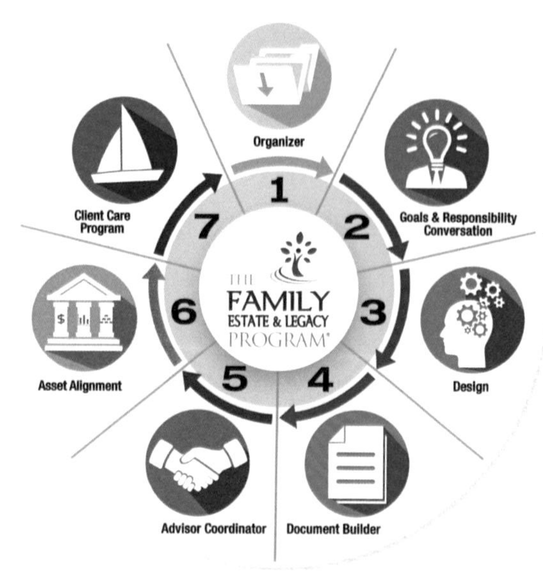

Hopefully these pages have encouraged you to get the most out of your estate plan. If you are interested in beginning your Family Estate & Legacy Program® journey, please contact our office to receive your Initial Client Package. We will send you an email to get things started and ask that you complete three easy steps:

Attend Our Workshop or Watch the Video

Our firm gives workshops several times a year outlining important and relevant estate planning issues we want you to consider and be prepared to discuss at our initial conference.

The initial client digital package contains a link to the video if you can't attend the workshop or if one isn't being provided soon. The video can be viewed on your laptop, tablet or smart phone.

Complete Your Client Organizer

It is important that we receive a completed Client Organizer at least three business days prior to our initial conference. The information you provide us is confidential and is very important in order for us to provide you proper legal advice. We can forward you a hard copy of the Client Organizer, or a digital one is available with the Initial Client package email you can download and print out to complete.

Drop Off or Email us Copies of Your Current Planning Documents

When getting us your Client Organizer, please also either drop-off copies or email PDF copies of your:

- Current will;
- Trust with any amendments;
- Irrevocable trusts;
- Federal Gift Tax Returns Form 709, if applicable;
- Federal Estate Tax Return Form 706 for your spouse, if applicable

If you don't have access to all of these documents, please get us what you can. Please email us a PDF copy that would be preferred. If not, we will scan in these items and return them to you.

Acknowledgments

Writing a "short" book on Florida residency and estate planning is difficult in the sense that one could write an entire treatise on the subject. I am grateful to my law partners, Hugh Kinsey, Jr., Michael B. Hill and Hayley E. Donaldson who provided insight, and to, our trusted associate, Andrew Barnett, who took burdens off me so that I could finish this project.

My very capable estate planning staff, including Maria Reimer, Dorothy Berry, Regina Sadoski, Aimee Balcer, Debbie Shannon and Bronwyn Merhige kept files moving while Maureen Phillips made sure the network hummed along. Donald V. (DJ) Wik, Jr. and Hayden Heidbreder of my team were instrumental in the design, layout and editing of this book.

Finally, I wish to express my love and appreciation for my wife, Patti, who endures the endless tippity taps of my laptop when I should be paying attention to her and the rest of the family.

About the Author

Craig R. Hersch

Craig R. Hersch is a Florida Bar Board Certified Wills, Trusts & Estates attorney, CPA, and is a founding shareholder and originating board member of a private trust company in Fort Myers, Florida. Mr. Hersch is a principal in his law firm, and has created several trademarked processes tied to his estate planning and administration practice, including The Family Estate & Legacy Program, The Estate Settlement Program, The Advanced Planning Expander™ and The Transitional Event Sequence™. All of these unique processes are designed to provide his clients comfort and clarity when navigating the complex legal, tax and financial concerns associated with planning and administering an estate.

In addition to this book, Hersch has authored *Common Cents Estate Planning*, *Legal Matters When a Loved One Dies*, *Selecting Your Trustee*, *Asset Alignment and Your Estate Plan*, *Common Cents Estate Planning II* and *The Estate Planner's Guide to Practice Development*. His work has appeared in several professional journals, including The Practical Tax Lawyer, Trusts & Estates Magazine, and The Florida Bar Journal. Hersch has been a featured lecturer at continuing education programs sponsored by the Florida Bar, the Florida Institute of CPAs, The Estate Planning Councils of Lee & Charlotte Counties and The National Business Institute.

Mr. Hersch writes a nationally published column on practice development for wealthmanagement.com, a web site produced by *Trusts & Estates Magazine*, a prestigious trade journal for lawyers, CPAs and trust officers. His also a member of *Trusts & Estates Magazine* Editorial Advisory Board on The Modern Practice. Moreover, he authors a weekly estate planning column geared to laymen published in Sanibel's Island Sun newspaper and which appears on his firm's blog at floridaestateplanning.com/blog.

He is married to wife Patti, and has three daughters, Gabrielle, Courtney and Madison of whom he is very proud.

Estate Planning Mindset Scorecard

Turn the page to see the Mindset Scorecard and read through the statements for each mindset. Score yoruself based on where your mindset falls on the spectrum. Place each column's score in the column to the far right and add it at the bottom.

Review the scores and contemplate what scores you would like to have when moving forward with the estate planning process.

Compare your scores with the ideal scores to see where you'd like to be before deciding tom ove forward with your estate plan.

Visit **floridaestateplanning.com/moreguide** or **turn to the last page of the book** to see your mindset results!

YOUR MINDSET QUIZ

	MINDSET	2 POINTS	5 POINTS
1	**TRANSPARENT THINKING** Are you willing to share your goals and concerns with us?	You see no point in sharing your goals, concerns, family, and financial situation with your legal team.	You're reluctant to share your goals, concerns, family and financial situation, giving your legal team only what they ought to know.
2	**RELATIONSHIP DRIVEN** How do you view your relationship with your legal team?	You consider your estate plan to be a simple transaction that should be a one-time event every ten or fifteen years.	You believe that you should update your estate plan every few years, and that one lawyer is as good as the next.
3	**RECEPTIVE** Are you receptive to your lawyer's ideas?	You know exactly what you want in an estate plan and consider online document preparation as good as what any attorney could do.	You believe that a good lawyer may have some useful ideas, but most of those won't apply to your situation anyway.
4	**RESPONSIVE** How responsive are you to your legal team's requests for information?	You suspect that your legal team only asks for asset and family information so that they can charge higher fees.	You decide what information your legal team needs and provide them only what you consider absolutely necessary.
5	**APPRECIATE PROCESS** Do you consider estate planning a simple transaction or a useful process?	You believe that estate planning is a one-step transaction that doesn't require much thought.	You're willing to answer a few questions, but become annoyed with all the steps your attorney asks of you.
6	**TEAM ORIENTED** Do you value interacting with a competent, well-trained estate planning team?	Since you are paying the attorney you expect only him to answer all of your questions. You won't interact with his team.	You're reluctant to share your goals, concerns, family and financial situation, giving your legal team only what they ought to know.
7	**RECOGNIZES EXPERTISE** Do you view all attorneys as having roughly the same skills and expertise?	You believe that most attorneys are interchangeable, and there's not much difference between them.	You reluctantly work with your attorney's team when you have to, but would prefer that you speak directly with him on most matters.
8	**EXPECTATIONS** What are your expectations regarding turnaround time and fees?	You expect all of your work to be completed yesterday, at little cost and done perfectly.	While you recognize that some attorneys are better than others, you don't believe you need the best for your situation.
	SCORECARD	► ► ► ► ►	► ► ► ► ►

8 POINTS	11 POINTS	SCORE NOW	FUTURE SCORE
You'll consider sharing your goals, concerns, family, and financial situation an imposition so you'll describe what you can with minimal effort.	You're eager to share your goals, concerns, family, and financial situation with your legal team, understanding that's the backbone to a successful plan.		
You agree that your plan should be monitored to keep up with the times, and see the value of having an ongoing relationship with a good firm.	You consider your legal team an important element of your legal, tax and financial relationships necessary to keep up with an ever changing world.		
You see how your lawyer's ideas might add value to your estate plan, but believe that's more to benefit your children and has little effect on you or your spouse.	You're open and receptive to our expertise in suggesting creative solutions leading to family harmony and protecting your financial well being.		
You understand your legal team knows what information is required, and are willing to provide it when you have the time.	You promptly and fully respond to your legal team's requests for information and feedback.		
You understand that good estate planning necessitates a thorough process, but haven't been exposed to working within one.	You appreciate that we have an organized, 7-module process to ensure the best design, implementation, and maintenance of your estate plan.		
You're willing to interact with your attorney's team, but need continuing assurances they are competent.	You are encouraged that our well trained team includes drafting and funding professionals who help your attorney serve you quickly and efficiently.		
You feel that you need a qualified attorney but aren't quite sure how to differentiate one firm from the other	You want experienced board certified specialists who can provide comfort and clarity in achieving your objectives.		
You have reasonable expectations regarding the time, value, and complexity of your matters in relation to fees.	You have high expectations that the estate planning experience and corresponding result will far exceed the price.		
▶ ▶ ▶ ▶ ▶	▶ ▶ ▶ ▶ ▶		

MINDSET QUIZ SCORING

THE DO-IT-YOURSELFER

You view the creation of a will or trust package as a simple transaction that should not take much time or effort. If you choose to work with a law firm, you may be happiest looking for a firm with a steeply discounted rate structure – that usually means a "one size fits all" estate plan, which you feel is adequate. You may be happiest working within a web-based online document preparation resource or with a generalist lawyer who is adept at putting together simple wills.

SCORE < 28

THE MINIMALIST CLIENT

While you may seek a law firm to assist you with your estate plan, you believe that your situation is simple and routine. You don't believe that a highly qualified estate planning attorney can add much value to your situation, so you're not looking to establish a long-term relationship with any particular lawyer or law firm. You are most content getting the transaction accomplished with as little effort on your part as possible. You may be quite satisfied working with a low level law associate or working directly with a paralegal at a firm that caters to clients who share this viewpoint.

SCORE 28-51

ESTATE PLANNING

THE SIGNATURE CLIENT

Congratulations! Your mindset is open to get the most out of your estate planning experience! You are a good candidate for working within our firm's seven-step unique process, THE FAMILY ESTATE & LEGACY PROGRAM® to address your concerns and achieve your goals. You can easily envision the value created by having a team guided by board certified trust and estate attorneys open your eyes to opportunities that you didn't know existed and taking the steps necessary to protect yourself and your loved ones when navigating the ever-changing will, trust and tax laws. You seek a long-term relationship with a highly qualified and specialized estate planning firm that will provide you and your loved ones with comfort and clarity now and into the future.

SCORE 52-75

THE TRANSFORMATIVE CLIENT

Congratulations! Your mindset is the highest attainable and is likely to result in a successful estate planning experience! You'll soon realize the value of working within our seven-step unique process, THE FAMILY ESTATE & LEGACY PROGRAM® created by board certified attorneys specializing in estates and trusts. You can easily envision how a team of trained professionals can provide comfort and clarity while adding continuing value as your estate plan adjusts to an ever changing legal, tax and financial world in addition to meeting the needs of evolving family dynamics. Further, you want to build a relationship with our highly qualified team giving you and subsequent generations of your family a strong group of trusted advisors to rely upon. You'll be intrigued with the various options that you may not have known existed, often resulting in tax savings for you and your loved ones, as well as protecting their inheritance from a variety of dangers.

SCORE > 75